AMERICAN-SWEDISH HANDBOOK

Eleventh Edition

Edited by
Christopher Olsson
Ruth McLaughlin

Swedish Council of America
2600 Park Avenue
Minneapolis, Minnesota 55407
Telephone: (612)871-0593
Telefax: (612)871-8682

ISBN 0-9609620-2-6

Table of Contents

Preface

The *American-Swedish Handbook* is published by Swedish Council of America to be a handy reference guide for persons interested in the Swedish heritage in America and in the relations between the countries of Sweden and the United States.

Ambassador Franklin Forsberg

The *Handbook* includes information on U.S. and Swedish diplomatic and consular offices, as well as the structure and activities of such agencies as the Swedish Information Service and the Swedish Tourist Board, and a listing of Swedish-American organizations around the countries, many of which are formally affiliated with the Council. It lists American educational institutions with Swedish roots and provides information on schools and other institutions that offer instruction in the Swedish language. *The Handbook* also suggests avenues for obtaining books in Swedish or books about Sweden and Swedish America.

This is the eleventh edition of the *American-Swedish Handbook* and the third that has been published by Swedish Council of America. The first eight editions were issued by the Augustana Swedish Institute of Rock Island, Illinois. When that organization disbanded, the project was transferred to the Council. The 9th edition was published in 1982 and a tenth edition came out in 1987. It is the intention of the Council to revise and continue publishing this valuable resource every 3-5 years.

The current volume is the responsibility of the Council's Publications Committee, under the leadership of Lennart Johansson. A number of volunteer editors have helped in shaping the various chapters. Our thanks go especially to Marna Feldt, Eric Lund, Mariann Tiblin, and to the many other individuals and organizations that responded to our questionnaires and other requests for information. My personal thanks go to the other directors of Swedish Council of America who recognize that the *American-Swedish Handbook* is a valuable resource for all people who treasure the Swedish heritage in America and who work to improve the relationship between the United States and Sweden.

Franklin Forsberg
Ambassador (ret.)
Chairman
Swedish Council of America

Swedish Council of America

Swedish Council of America was founded nearly twenty years ago to bring into a cooperative relationship all organizations that work to celebrate the Swedish heritage in the United States and to strengthen the cultural relationship between Sweden and America.

The Council's activities are many. It has published several books, including Allan Kastrup's *The Swedish Heritage in America* and the collection of essays called *Partners in Progress*. This *Handbook* is the third edition of the *American-Swedish Handbook* it has issued.

The Council's leadership during the New Sweden '88 celebration led to the production and distribution of a major exhibit *Sweden and America 1638-1988: A History Celebrated* and the videotape "Sweden & America, 350 Years of Friendship".

The 119 organizations affiliated with Swedish Council of America receive regular mailings of information on upcoming cultural events and other offerings visiting from Sweden, as well as updates on cultural resources available in this country. In 1989 in St. Louis, Missouri, and in 1990 in Dearborn, Michigan, the Council sponsored a "Conference of Swedish America", each a weekend of seminars, workshops, and a 'resources fair' for delegates from the Council's affiliated organizations.

Every two years the Council presents the Great Swedish Heritage Award to distinguished and deserving Americans of Swedish descent and honors a Swedish citizen with "America's Swede of the Year" Award. The Council maintains a modest grants program to support projects that further the aims of the Council. In an effort to increase the resources available to worthy programs, the Council launched "The Campaign to Preserve the Swedish Heritage in America" in 1990. This fund raising campaign will establish an endowment fund, the income from which will allow the Grants Committee to support more fully many programs and projects in all parts of Swedish America.

Most Swedish-Americans know about Swedish Council of America through receiving the Council's quarterly magazine **Sweden & America.** This publication is sent to ca. 30,000 Swedish-American households around the country. It presents articles about the people and culture of Sweden and Swedish America as well as news about Swedish-American organizations and personalities.

The Council is governed by a board of directors elected by the organization's participatory groups and maintains offices and staff at the American Swedish Institute in Minneapolis. It was chartered in the State of Minnesota in 1972 and is exempt from federal income taxes under Section 501(c)(3) of the Internal Revenue Code.

Directors of Swedish Council of America

Franklin S. Forsberg	*chairman*
Roy A. Anderson	*vice-chairman*
Glen E. Brolander	*vice-chairman*
Siri Eliason	*vice-chairman*
Nils Hasselmo	*vice-chairman*
Birger Jansson	*vice-chairman*
Lennart N. Johansson	*vice-chairman*
Bertil O. Lundh	*vice-chairman*
John Sellstrom	*secretary*
Duane Kullberg	*treasurer*
Gerald E. Anderson	
Philip J. Anderson	
Wendell R. Anderson	
Thomas R. Bolling	
Donald R. Borgeson	
Ann Barton Brown	
Curtis L. Carlson	*chairman emeritus*
Robert J. Carlson	
Robert A. Falk	
Philip Graham	
E. Jan Hartmann	
Maynard B. Hasselquist	
William E. Hoglund	
G. Timothy Johnson	
Herbert F. Johnson	
LeRoy M. Johnson	
Bruce Karstadt	
David LaVine	
O. Greg Linde	
Edward A. Lindell	
Richard T. Lindgren	
Wendell Lund	
Oscar A. Lundin	*chairman emeritus*
Patricia McFate	
Michael L. Miller	
Agneta Nilsson	

George A. Nord
Byron Nordstrom
Alan J. Olson
George Orescan
Gerald Pearson
Robert A. Peterson
Rudolph A. Peterson
Lawrence Plym
Robert Roosa
Glenn T. Seaborg   *chairman emeritus*
Henry T. Segerstrom
Lloyd O. Swanson
Nils William Olsson   *director emeritus/founding executive director*
Nils Y. Wessell   *director emeritus/founding president*

Affiliated organizations of Swedish Council of America

PARTICIPATORY GROUPS

▲ American Swedish Historical Museum	Philadelphia, PA
▲ The American Swedish Institute	Minneapolis, MN
▲ Detroit-Swedish Council, Inc.	Detroit, MI
▲ Swedish-American Historical Society	Chicago, IL

AFFILIATE GROUPS

▲ Agassiz Swedish Heritage Society	Warren, MN
▲ American Daughters of Sweden	Chicago, IL
▲ American Friends of the Emigrant Institute of Sweden, Inc.	East Moline, IL
▲ American Scandinavian Association at Augustana	Rock Island, IL
▲ American-Scandinavian Association of the Great Plains	Lindsborg, KS
▲ American Scandinavian Heritage Foundation, Inc.	Jamestown, NY
▲ The American Society of Swedish Engineers	New York, NY
▲ The American Swedish Institute—Bemidji Affiliate	Bemidji, MN
▲ American Union of Swedish Singers	Des Plaines, IL
▲ Augustana College	Rock Island, IL

- ▲ Augustana Historical Society — Rock Island, IL
- ▲ Bethany College — Lindsborg, KS
- ▲ Bethel College & Seminary — St. Paul, MN
- ▲ Bishop Hill Heritage Association — Bishop Hill, IL
- ▲ The Cadillac Area Scandinavian Society — Cadillac, MI
- ▲ Carl Sandburg Historic Site Association — Wataga, IL
- ▲ The Central Swedish Committee of Chicago — Rockford, IL
- ▲ Dalesburg Scandinavian Association — Centerville, SD
- ▲ The Delaware Swedish Colonial Society — Wilmington, DE
- ▲ Des Moines Associates of the American Scandinavian Foundation — Des Moines, IA
- ▲ Emigrant Register — Karlstad, Sweden
- ▲ FEST! — Minneapolis, MN
- ▲ Folklife Institute of Central Kansas — Lindsborg, KS
- ▲ Friends of Scandinavia — Raleigh, NC
- ▲ Gammelgården — Scandia, MN
- ▲ Gustavus Adolphus College — St. Peter, MN
- ▲ Heritage Institute of Ellis Island — New York, NY
- ▲ House of Sweden — San Diego, CA
- ▲ Independent Order of Vikings — Des Plaines, IL
- ▲ Jamestown Community College — Jamestown, NY
- ▲ The Jenny Lind Club of Detroit — Detroit, MI
- ▲ Kichi-Saga Swedish Club — Lindstrom, MN
- ▲ Kingsburg District Chamber of Commerce — Kingsburg, CA
- ▲ Kittson County Historical Society — Lake Bronson, MN
- ▲ Lake Regions Swedish Heritage Society — Devils Lake, ND
- ▲ The Linneas of Texas — Houston, TX
- ▲ The Midwest Institute of Scandinavian Culture — Èau Claire, WI
- ▲ New Sweden Cultural Heritage Society of Oregon & Washington — Portland, OR
- ▲ New Sweden Farmstead/Museum — Bridgeton, NJ
- ▲ New Sweden Historical Society — New Sweden, ME
- ▲ The Noon Day Scandinavian Club — Omaha, NE
- ▲ Norden Club of Jamestown, NY — Jamestown, NY
- ▲ Norden Women's Club — Jamestown, NY
- ▲ Nordic Heritage Museum — Seattle, WA
- ▲ North Park College — Chicago, IL
- ▲ Northwest Iowa Associates of the American-Scandinavian Foundation — Peterson, IA

- Oakland Chamber of Commerce — Oakland, NE
- Ozarks Scandinavian Society of Springfield, Missouri — Springfield, MO
- Positive Sweden — Mill Valley, CA
- The Raoul Wallenberg Committee of the United States, Ltd. — New York, NY
- Riksföreningen Sverigekontakt — Gothenburg, Sweden
- San Antonio Scandinavians — San Antonio, TX
- Scandinavian American Foundation of Georgia — Decatur, GA
- Scandinavian Club of Greater Kansas City — Kansas City, MO
- Scandinavian Cultural Council of Pacific Lutheran University — Tacoma, WA
- Scandinavian Cultural Society of Greater Hartford — West Hartford, CT
- Scandinavian Heritage Group — Gothenburg, NE
- Scandinavian Society of Greater Lansing — Lansing, MI
- The Scandinavian Society of Wichita — Wichita, KS
- Scandinavian Studies Department, University of Minnesota — Minneapolis, MN
- Stockholm Historical Society — Stockholm, ME
- SVEA (Swedish Women's Association of Chicago) — Chicago, IL
- SVEA of Texas — Bellaire, TX
- SVEA, Washington, DC, Inc. — Washington, DC
- Sveaborg — Baltimore, MD
- Svenska Vänner — Jamestown, ND
- Svenska Vännerna, Inc. — Sherburn, MN
- SWEA International, Inc. — Portola Valley, CA
- Swedish-American Chamber of Commerce, Inc., (Houston Chapter) — Houston, TX
- Swedish-American Chamber of Commerce, Inc., (New York Chapter) — New York, NY
- Swedish-American Chamber of Commerce of the Western United States — San Francisco, CA
- The Swedish American Council of Boston — Boston, MA
- Swedish-American Cultural Union — Washington, DC
- Swedish American Historical Association of California — Los Angeles, CA
- The Swedish American Museum Center of Chicago — Chicago, IL
- The Swedish Club — Houston, TX
- Swedish Club — Seattle, WA

- The Swedish Club of Denver · Denver, CO
- Swedish Club of Los Angeles · Los Angeles, CA
- Swedish Club of Metropolitan Detroit · Farmington Hills, MI
- Swedish Club of San Francisco and Bay Area · San Francisco, CA
- Swedish Club of Sarasota · Sarasota, FL
- The Swedish Colonial Society · Philadelphia, PA
- Swedish Conversation Club · Iowa City, IA
- Swedish Council of St. Louis · St. Louis, MO
- Swedish Cultural Committee · Omaha, NE
- The Swedish Cultural Heritage Society of the
  Red River Valley · Fargo, ND
- Swedish Cultural Society in America · St. Paul, MN
- Swedish Cultural Society of Cleveland · Cleveland, OH
- Swedish Cultural Society of Rockford · Rockford, IL
- Swedish Culture Society · Largo, FL
- Swedish Emigrant Institute · Växjö, Sweden
- Swedish Heritage Center · Oakland, NE
- Swedish Heritage Society · Swedesburg, IA
- Swedish Heritage Society of Northern Colorado · Greeley, CO
- Swedish Heritage Society of Utah, Inc. · Salt Lake City, UT
- Swedish Historical Society of Rockford · Rockford, IL
- Swedish Northern Lights Society · Grand Rapids, MN
- Swedish Press Society · Vancouver, BC, Canada
- Swenson Swedish Immigration Research Center · Rock Island, IL
- Södra Vätterbygdens Folkhögskola · Jönköping, Sweden
- Texas Swedish Cultural Foundation, Inc. · Houston, TX
- Three Crowns American Swedish Association · Bismarck, ND
- Tre Kronor Scandinavian Society · Holdrege, NE
- United Swedish Societies of New York · New York, NY
- Upsala College · East Orange, NJ
- Vasa Order of America, Carl Larsson Lodge · Raleigh, NC
- Vasa Order of America, Drott Lodge · Washington, DC
- Vasa Order of America, Grand Lodge · Cranston, RI
- Vasa Order of America, Svea Lodge · Indianapolis, IN
- Vasa Order of America, Valhalla Lodge · Las Vegas, NV
- Vasa Order of America, Viking Lodge · Millington, MI
- Värmlands Vännerna · New York, NY
- West Shore Scandinavian Society · Ludington, MI
- Western Carolinas Association of the
  American Scandinavian Foundation · Hendersonville, NC

GOVERNMENTAL AND QUASI-GOVERNMENTAL AGENCIES

U.S. Diplomatic and Consular Representation in Sweden

The American Embassy

Strandvägen 101
S-115 89 Stockholm, Sweden
Tel. 08 783 53 00
Fax 08 661 19 64

      Charles E. Redman, Ambassador

      Michael Klosson, Chargé d'Affaires
      George F. Beasley, Counselor for Press and Cultural Affairs
      Andrea J. Nelson, Counselor for Administrative Affairs
      Harrison Sherwood, Counselor for Commercial Affairs
      Kenneth H. Kolb, Counselor for Economic Affairs
      Thomas R. Hanson, Counselor for Political Affairs

      John L. Golden, Defense and Air Attaché
      Colonel Carl-Gustav Finström, Army Attaché
      Robert M. Hanson, Naval Attaché
      Gordon S. Nicks, Agricultural Attaché
      Beatrice A. Camp, First Secretary for Information Affairs
      Brian H. Guss, First Secretary for Cultural Affairs

Swedish Diplomatic and Consular Representation in the United States

Embassy of Sweden
Watergate 600, Suite 1200
600 New Hampshire Avenue N.W.
Washington, DC 20037
Tel. (202)944-5600
Fax (202)342-1319

Anders Thunborg, Ambassador
Sven-Olof Petersson, Minister

Political Section
Staffan Carlsson, Counselor
Annika Jagander, First Secretary

Economic Section
Percy Westerlund, Minister Economic Affairs
Lars-Olof G. Hollner, First Secretary
Ulf Lindell, Second Secretary
Lars F.V. Bjerde, Counselor, (Defense Procurement)
Per-Anders Hallqvist, Second Secretary

Culture and Information Section
Lars Romert, Press Counselor
Ingmar Björkstén, Cultural Counselor
Lena Kjellström, Second Secretary

Administrative and Consular Section
Alf Karlsson, Counselor
Agneta Bergman, Second Secretary

Military Section
Brigadier General Per-Arne Ringh, Defense and Military Attaché
Colonel Karl-Göte Widén, Defense and Naval Attaché
Captain Christer Hägg, Naval Attaché
Major Karl-Gustav Bartoll, Asst. Military Attaché
Colonel Bo Gellerhed, Asst. Naval and Air Attaché

Special Attachés
Svante Lundin, Counselor, Science and Technology
Anders Lundin, Counselor, Agricultural Affairs
Carin Walldin, Counselor, Labor Affairs

Swedish Consulates
Consulates General

New York

Consulate General of Sweden
One Dag Hammarskjold Plaza, 45th floor
New York, NY 10017-2201
Tel. (212)751-5900
Fax (212)755-2732

Consul General: Arne Thorén

Chicago

Consulate General of Sweden
150 N. Michigan Avenue, Suite 1250
Chicago, IL 60601-7593
Tel. (312)781-6262
Fax (312)704-8262

Consul General: Lave Johnsson
Consul: Rolf Sandling

Los Angeles

Consulate General of Sweden
10880 Wilshire Boulevard, Suite 505
Los Angeles, CA 90024-4314
Tel. (213)470-2555
Fax (213)475-4683

Consul General: Peter Hammarström

Honorary Consulates under the jurisdiction of the Consulate General in New York.

Atlanta

Consulate of Sweden
Atlanta Financial Center
3333 Peachtree Road, N.E., Suite 1420 E
Atlanta, GA 30326
Tel. (404)261-1187
Fax (404)266-8677

Consul: Holcombe T. Green, Jr.
Assistant: Anette Odom

District: The state of Georgia, except the city of Savannah.

Baltimore

    Consulate of Sweden
    10 North Calvert Street, Suite L-45
    Baltimore, MD 21202
    Tel. (301)539-5061
    Fax (301)539-5055

    Consul: Charles E. Scarlett, III
    Assistant: Kathy Hawkins

    District: The state of Maryland

Boston

    Consulate of Sweden
    6 St. James Avenue, Suite 1001
    Boston, MA 02116-3845
    Tel. (617)426-5558
    Fax (617)542-3304

    Consul: Wendell N. Gustafson
    Chancellor: Britt Ahlfert
    Administrative Assistant: Margareta Andrews

    District: The commonwealth of Massachusetts

Buffalo

    Consulate of Sweden
    Gould & Swanson, P.C.
    1800 Liberty Building
    Buffalo, NY 14202-3686
    Tel. (716)854-3110
    Fax (716)854-1113

    Consul: Roger G. Swanson

    District: The counties of Erie, Genesee, Livingston, Monroe,
    Niagara, Orleans, and Wyoming in the state of New York.

Charlotte Amalie, Virgin Islands

    (Vacant)

Fort Lauderdale and Miami

    Consulate of Sweden
    Howard Amman Building
    611 Eisenhower Boulevard, 3rd floor
    PO Box 13094
    Fort Lauderdale, FL 33316
    Tel. (305)467-3507
    Fax (305)462-5788

Consul: John I. Tureman, Jr.
Vice Consul: Gunilla Lundström-North

District: The state of Florida, except counties of Duval, Nassau, Hillsborough, and Pinellas.

Hamilton, Bermuda

Consulate of Sweden
Boyle Building, Queen Street
PO Box HM 1554
Hamilton 5-31 Bermuda
Tel. (809)292-8369
Fax (809)292-5892

Consul: W. Neville Conyers
Chancellor: Judy Craig

District: The Bermuda Islands

Jacksonville

Consulate of Sweden
c/o Sandwell Inc.
9424 Baymeadows Road, Suite 100
Jacksonville, FL 32256
Tel. (904)739-0313
Fax (904)739-3986

Consul: Lennart Jansson

District: The counties of Duval and Nassau in the state of Florida.

Jamestown

Consulate of Sweden
9-11 East Fourth Street
PO Box 50
Jamestown, NY 14701-0050
Tel. (716)484-7191
Fax (716)484-2133

Consul: John L. Sellstrom

District: The city of Jamestown in the state of New York.

Mobile

Consulate of Sweden
2256 Ashland Place Avenue
Mobile, AL 36607
Tel. (205)829-4047 ext. 2115
Fax (205)944-2201

Consul: Richard W. Overbey

District: The state of Alabama

New Orleans

Consulate of Sweden
Strachan Shipping Co.
2640 Canal Street
New Orleans, LA 70119
Tel. (504)827-8711
Fax (504)827-8792

Consul: William B. Forsyth

District: The states of Louisiana and Mississippi

Norfolk

Consulate of Sweden
201 East City Hall Avenue
PO Box 3430
Norfolk, VA 23510
Tel. (804)446-7300
Fax (804)625-7854

Consul: Rolf Williams

District: The commonwealth of Virginia

Philadelphia

Consulate of Sweden
112 Christian Street
Philadelphia, PA 19147
Tel. (215)465-5565
Fax (215)336-3389

Consul: Bengt O. Jansson

District: The commonwealth of Pennsylvania

Portland

Consulate of Sweden
465 Congress Street, Suite 108
Portland, ME 04101
Tel. (207)761-2526
Fax (207)761-1791

Consul: Martin R. Johnson

District: The state of Maine

San Juan, Puerto Rico

Consulate of Sweden
c/o Intership
Avenida Fernandez Juncos Muelle II
PO Box 2748
San Juan, PR 00903
Tel. (809)721-4355
Fax (809)721-4343

Consul: David R. Segarra, Jr.

District: The commonwealth of Puerto Rico

Savannah

Consulate of Sweden
1 Rockwell Avenue South
Savannah, GA 31419
Tel. (912)927-1126

Consul: Alexander Pratt Adams

District: The city of Savannah

St. Petersburg

Consulate of Sweden
Prudential Securities, Inc.
28100 U.S. Highway 19 North, Suite 100
Clearwater, FL 34621
Tel. (813)799-5540, 225-1075

Consul: Howard L. Hill

District: The counties of Hillsborough and Pinellas in the State of
Florida.

Honorary Consulates under the jurisdiction of the Consulate General in Chicago

Cleveland

Consulate of Sweden
1800 Society Building
East 9th and Superior
Cleveland, OH 44114-2688
Tel. (216)621-4995
Fax (216)241-0816

Consul: Michael L. Miller

District: The state of Ohio

Dallas

Consulate of Sweden
5956 Cherry Lane, Suite 1616
Dallas, TX 75225-6522
Tel. (214)363-0800
Fax (214)363-0924

Consul: J. Robert Alpert

District: The city of Dallas

Detroit

Consulate of Sweden
1290 East Maple Road
PO Box 1290
Troy, MI 48007-1290
Tel. (313)588-3310
Fax (313)588-0718

Consul: E. Jan Hartmann

District: The state of Michigan

Houston

Consulate General of Sweden
c/o Fowler International
4422 First City Tower
1001 Fannin Street
Houston, TX 77002-6778
Tel. (713)651-1617
Fax (713)651-9231

Consul General: Robert A. Fowler

Official Address of the Consulate General
5123 Bellaire Boulevard
Bellaire (Houston), TX 77401
Tel. (713)295-5747, 295-5755
Fax (713)667-7300

District: The state of Texas, with the exception of the city of
Dallas

Kansas City

Consulate of Sweden
J.C. Nichols Company
310 Ward Parkway
Kansas City, MO 64112
Tel. (816)561-3456
Fax (816)561-3456, ext. 211

Consul: Clarence L. Roeder

District: The state of Kansas and Kansas City, Missouri, as well as the counties of Cass, Clay, Jackson, and Platte in the state of Missouri.

Minneapolis

Consulate General of Sweden
720 Baker Bldg.
706 Second Avenue South
PO Box 2107
Minneapolis, MN 55402
Tel. (612)332-6897
Fax (612)724-1841

Consul General: Wendell R. Anderson

District: The state of Minnesota

Milwaukee

Consulate of Sweden
800 North Marshall Street
Milwaukee, WI 53202
Tel. (414)273-3393
Fax (414)273-1058

Consul: Anders S.C. Segerdahl

District: The state of Wisconsin

Omaha

Consulate of Sweden
One Merrill Lynch Plaza
10330 Regency Parkway Drive
Omaha, NE 68114
Tel. (402)397-2200
Fax (402)390-7137

Consul: Donald Erickson

Consulate of Sweden
700 Service Life Building
1904 Farnam Street
Omaha, NE 68102
Tel. (402)341-3333
Vice Consul: Thomas J. Lund

District: The state of Nebraska

St. Louis

Consulate of Sweden
501 North Broadway
PO Box 14020
St. Louis, MO 63178
Tel. (314)331-6591
Fax (314)331-6554

Consul: G. Richard Oscarson

District: The state of Missouri, with the exception of Kansas City, the counties of Cass, Clay, Jackson, and Platte. Also includes counties of Madison and St. Clair in the state of Illinois.

Honorary Consulates under the jurisdiction of the Consulate General in Los Angeles.

Anchorage

Consulate of Sweden
301 W. Northern Lights Boulevard
Anchorage, AK 99503

Mailing Address
PO Box 100-600
Anchorage, AK 99510-0600
Tel. (907)265-2927

Consul: Edward B. Rasmuson

District: The state of Alaska

Denver

Consulate of Sweden
2121 S. Oneida Street
Suite 525, Oneida Tower
Denver, CO 80224
Tel. (303)758-0999
Fax (303)758-1091

Consul: Glenn D. Peterson
Vice Consul: Donald Glenn Peterson

District: The states of Colorado, New Mexico, and Wyoming

Honolulu

Consulate of Sweden
Grosvenor Center
737 Bishop Street, Suite 2600
Honolulu, HI 96813

Mailing Address
PO Box 494
Honolulu, HI 96809-0494
Tel. (808)528-4777
Office Tel. (808)547-5400
Fax (808)523-1920

Consul: James M. Cribley
Assistant: Ingrid Scheerer

District: The state of Hawaii

Phoenix

Consulate of Sweden
9200 N Central Avenue
Phoenix, AZ 85020

Mailing Address
PO Box 9957
Phoenix, AZ 85068
Tel. (602)997-0977

Consul: Russell O. Allen

District: The state of Arizona

Portland

Consulate of Sweden
1600 S.W. Fourth Avenue
Portland, OR 97201

Mailing Address
PO Box 8699
Portland, OR 97207
Tel. (503)224-4155
Fax (503)274-2155

Consul: Leonard Forsgren

District: The state of Oregon

San Diego

Consulate of Sweden
530 Broadway, Suite 1106
San Diego, CA 92101
Tel. (619)233-1106
Fax (619)233-9890

Consul: John H. Norton

District: The city of San Diego

San Francisco

Consulate General of Sweden
120 Montgomery Street, Suite 2175
San Francisco, CA 94104
Tel. (415)788-2631
Fax (415)982-7362

Consul General: Siri Eliason

District: The city of San Francisco and the counties of Alameda, Contra Costa, Marin, Napa, San Mateo, Santa Clara, Solano, and Sonoma.

Seattle

Consulate of Sweden
1020 Joseph Vance building
3rd Avenue and Union Street
Seattle, WA 98101
Tel. (206)622-5640
Fax (206)273-1058

Consul: Clifford C. Benson
Chancellor: Lennart Åkerlund

District: The state of Washington

The Swedish Information Service in the United States (SIS)

One Dag Hammarskjold Plaza
New York, NY 10017-2201
Tel. (212)751-5900
Fax (212)752-4789

Director   Torsten Nilsson

Purpose   The Swedish Information Service is a unit of the Swedish Ministry for Foreign Affairs, responsible to the Embassy in Washington, DC, and working in close cooperation with the consulates general in the United States and Canada. The purpose of SIS is to provide a central resource for all persons and organizations seeking information about Sweden on subjects other than tourism and trade/business.

Activities   SIS maintains a library with a wide variety of materials, ranging from current Swedish newspapers and periodicals to extensive reference works, available for researchers, scholars, and the media as well as for the casual visitor. The documentation section stocks hundreds of different pamphlets, pocket books, fact sheets, and brochures in English dealing with practically every aspect of life in Sweden. To stimulate cultural and technical exchange, a series of seminars have been established jointly with the embassies and consulates general in the United States and Canada. The purpose is to bring together Swedish and local professionals to trade views and ideas within their areas of specialization. The topics are focused on current debate. Cooperation with American colleges and universities plays an important role in the overall program of the Swedish Information Service, especially with those institutions offering courses in the Swedish language and in Scandinavian political, social, and literary studies. When projects call for contacts in Sweden or specialized material not available at SIS, the requests are channeled to the Swedish Institute in Stockholm, which is also responsible for arranging programs for visiting professionals. SIS also endeavors to bring guest lecturers from Sweden to university audiences and other interested groups. Photographs, videos and 16mm films, slide talks, and special exhibit materials are available. SIS also circulates exhibits produced by the Swedish Institute and other organizations.

Publications SIS publishes *Viewpoint Sweden*, a series of bulletins providing background and opinions by Swedish and American authors on issues of public interest. Releases about special events and news items are included among SIS's publications.

Other Offices

San Francisco
120 Montgomery Street, Suite 2107
San Francisco, CA 94104
Tel. (415)788-2631
Fax (415)982-7362

Ulla Wikander-Reilly
Karin Seeman
Information Officers

Los Angeles
10880 Wilshire Boulevard, Suite 505
Los Angeles, CA 90024
Tel. (213)470-2555
Fax (213)475-4683

Kjell Holm, Press Attaché

Swedish Trade Councils in the United States

Swedish Trade Council

150 N. Michigan Avenue, Suite 1200
Chicago, IL 60601
Tel. (312)781-6222
Fax (312)346-0683

Göran Rännefors
Trade Commissioner to the United States

Swedish Trade Council

c/o Swedish-American Chamber of Commerce
599 Lexington Avenue, 42nd floor
New York, NY 10022
Tel. (212)838-5530
Fax (212)755-7953

Olle Wijkstrom
Trade Commissioner

Swedish Trade Council

10880 Wilshire Boulevard, Suite 914
Los Angeles, CA 90024
Tel. (213)475-2215
Fax (213)475-0591

Stellan Linton
Trade Commissioner

Swedish Trade Council

300 Park, Suite 265
Birmingham, MI 48009
Tel. (313)644-3599
Fax (313)644-5329

Åke Blomgren
Deputy Trade Commissioner

Swedish Trade Council

235 Peachtree Street N.E.
1801 Gas Light Tower
Atlanta, GA 30303
Tel. (404)223-0374
Fax (404)522-2136

Per Olof Palm
Trade Commissioner

Travel to and from Scandinavia

Travelers to Sweden may obtain a wide variety of information sheets, maps, local tourist fact sheets, etc. from the Swedish Tourist Board in New York. Specific arrangements for travel to Sweden and Scandinavia should be made directly with the air carriers serving that part of the world or through your local travel agency.

Swedish Tourist Board

> 655 Third Avenue
> New York, NY 10017
> Tel. (212)949-2333
> Fax (212)697-0835

Scandinavian Tourist Boards

> 150 N. Michigan Avenue
> Chicago, IL 60601
> Tel. (312)726-1120
>
> 8929 Wilshire Blvd.
> Beverly Hills, CA 90211
> Tel. (213)657-4808

Swedish Tourist Board, head office:

> Sveriges Turistråd
> Sverigehuset
> Box 7473
> S-103 92 Stockholm
> Sweden
> Tel. 011 46 8 789 20 00
> Fax 011 46 8 21 35 55

U.S. Passport:

> Contact the U.S. passport agency nearest you or your local post office.

Air transportation:

> The following airlines currently serve Scandinavian, either directly or through other European ports of entry:
>
> ▲ American Airlines 1-800-624-6262
> direct flight from **Chicago** to **Stockholm**
>
> ▲ Finnair 1-800-950-5000
> from **New York**
> via Helsinki to **Stockholm**

▲ Icelandair 1-800-223-5500
from **New York, Baltimore,** or **Orlando**
via Reykjavik
to **Copenhagen, Gothenburg,** or **Stockholm**

▲ KLM Royal Dutch Airlines 1-800-777-5553
from **Atlanta, Baltimore, Chicago, Houston, Minneapolis/
St.Paul, New York,** or **Orlando**
via Amsterdam
to **Copenhagen, Gothenburg, Malmö, Oslo, Stavanger,** or
Stockholm

▲ Scandinavian Airlines System 1-800-221-2350
direct flight from **New York** to **Oslo** or **Stockholm;**
from **Chicago, Los Angeles,** or **Seattle**
via Copenhagen
to **Gothenburg, Oslo, Stockholm**

▲ Trans World Airlines, Inc. 1-800-221-2000
direct flight from **New York** to **Copenhagen** or **Stockholm**

Stockholm City Hall.

NON-GOVERNMENTAL
ORGANIZATIONS

Non-governmental organizations and institutions

The organizations and institutions listed below include Swedish-American and Scandinavian-American groups, as well as other organizations—such as colleges, chambers of commerce, research institutes, and other organizations which promote the culture and heritage of Sweden and/or Scandinavia in the United States.

◆ Agassiz Swedish Heritage Society

c/o Evangeline Myhre, Newsletter Editor
705 E. Fletcher
Warren, MN 56762
Tel. (218)745-5447

President   Lyndon Johnson

Founded   April 1987

Members   279

Purpose   The purpose of the Society is for the members to preserve their heritage, learn about the Swedish culture and history, to have liaison with the people of Sweden and Swedish-Americans, and to have "good times" together doing so.

Activities   A St. Lucia fest; a talk on the American Swedish Institute by its director; a joint meeting with the Sons of Norway; a lecture by Dr. Lars Ljungmark, Swedish writer and historian on immigration from Sweden; recording all the churches started by Swedish immigrants; awarding two scholarships to attend the Concordia College Swedish Language Village.

Publication A newsletter published six times a year.

◆ American Daughters of Sweden

c/o Bernadine O'Connor
6373 Blackhawk Trail
Indian Head Park, IL 60525
Tel. (708)246-3349

President   Bernadine O'Connor

Founded   1926

Members   375

Purpose   The American Daughters of Sweden aim to keep alive and foster the heritage of Swedish culture, stimulate an intelligent interest in civic, educational, and social affairs that advances the welfare of local and national life, and unite Swedish women in America and in Sweden in closer bonds of sympathy and good fellowship.

Activities   A smörgåsbord, holiday bazaar, and a spring luncheon. They sponsor permanently endowed scholarships at the University of Chicago, Augustana College, and North Park College, and provide scholarships to the International Language Village in Minnesota.

Publications   A monthly newsletter; SWEDISH RECIPES OLD AND NEW, a cookbook.

◆ American Friends of the Emigrant Institute of Sweden, Inc.

c/o Lennart Setterdahl, Secretary
3452 Fourth Street
East Moline, IL 61244
Tel. (309)755-2858
Fax (309)755-1573

President   Gunnar Mossblad
              9951 Hascall Street
              Omaha, NE 68124
              Tel. (402)391-8910
              Fax (402)453-2082
Founded   1984
Members   13 (members of board and registered agent)

Purpose   To help preserve the Swedish-American heritage and promote research into Swedish immigration by locating, generating, and acquiring historical information on Swedish immigrants and their offspring. The research is mainly conducted through oral history projects. They have now interviewed over 1,200 Swedish-Americans and a portion of the collection is on deposit at the Emigrant Institute in Växjö.

Activities   Oral interviews conducted in Jamestown, NY, Rockford, IL, the Quad Cities area in IL, Kansas City, MO, and other localities; receptions for Swedish-American interviewees. The organization meets three to four times annually.

◆ American Scandinavian Association at Augustana College

c/o Roberta Anderson
2712 30th Street
Moline, IL 61265

President   Ordell W. Peterson

Founded   1933

Members   308

Purpose   The organization attempts to stimulate and promote interest in American-Scandinavian relations and the culture of the Scandinavian countries, and to preserve the Scandinavian heritage in the Western Illinois/Eastern Iowa area.

Activities   Membership tea; Scandinavian craft workshop; bus trips; concerts by Swedish musical groups; Scandinavian cooking school; Jul dinner; Midsommar festival; pea soup supper; St. Lucia festival and smörgåsbord; annual banquet and business meeting; sponsor a play at the Playcrafters Barn in Moline, IL; donate money for the purchase of art created by artists with Scandinavian heritage; Swedish classes; programs related to all five Scandinavian countries.

Publication   A bimonthly newsletter.

◆ American-Scandinavian Association of the Great Plains, Inc.

c/o A. John Pearson
PO Box 265
Lindsborg, KS 67456
Tel. (913)227-2302

President   DeVere Blomberg

Founded   October 12, 1973

Members   125

Purpose   The Association's purpose is to promote and strengthen the cultural, educational, and intellectual relations between the organization's region of the United States and Denmark, Finland, Iceland, Norway, and Sweden. It also desires to preserve the Scandinavian-American heritage and encourage the continued recognition and observation of Scandinavian customs and folklore; to sponsor and promote contemporary activities, concerts, and events to that end.

Activities   The organization sponsors and promotes contemporary lecturers, art exhibits of Scandinavian artists, and films. It helps sponsor Midsummer festivals and dinners, and St. Lucia and Christmas celebrations. Meetings are held approximately once every two months.

Publication A periodic newsletter.

The American Scandinavian Association of the National Capital Area, Inc.

c/o Mildred B. Hanson
3130 Eakin Park Court
Fairfax, VA 22031
Tel. (703)208-4253

President   Mildred B. Hanson

Founded   1983

Members   610

Purpose   The American Scandinavian Association of the National Capital Area, Inc., is the successor to the Washington, DC chapter of the American Scandinavian Foundation. ASA's goals are: to promote cultural exchange between the United States and Denmark, Finland, Iceland, Norway, and Sweden; to increase understanding and appreciation of the Nordic people among Americans; and to provide a forum where people of the area can meet and join others to enjoy Nordic culture and to socialize. ASA is a member of the Scandinavian Council of Washington, a joint committee of various Nordic ethnic societies, formed for common endeavors.

Activities   A Christmas - St. Lucia fest; a Midsummer picnic; an illustrated lecture: "The Baltic Sea—Fact and Fiction" by Captain Edward L. Beach; panel discussion: "The Nordic Countries and the European Community" by representatives of the Nordic embassies in Washington; "The Royal Danish Ballet - the Bournonville Tradition".

Publication A monthly newsletter.

Auxiliaries   The Scandinavian Literature Group
The Young Scandinavians

The American-Scandinavian Foundation (ASF)

725 Park Avenue
New York, NY 10021
Tel. (212)879-9779
Fax (212)249-3444

President   Lena Biörck Kaplan

Founded   1910

Members   5,000

Purpose   The purpose of ASF is educational and cultural exchange between the United States and Denmark, Finland, Iceland, Norway, and Sweden.

Activities   The organization holds programs throughout the year. Some of the activities include: trainee programs, art exhibits, fellowships and grants, film series, and lectures.

Publications SCANDINAVIAN REVIEW, a journal; SCAN, a newsletter, and an annual report.

Associate groups

◆ **American Scandinavian Association at Augustana College**
Roberta Anderson, Secretary
2712 30th Street
Moline, IL 61265
(309)764-4273 (Dr. Milford Nelson)

◆ **The American-Scandinavian Association
of the Great Plains**
Mr. DeVere Blomberg, President
216 West Bond
Salinas, KS 67401
(913)823-2246 (day)
(913)825-4154 (evening)

**The American Scandinavian Association
of the National Capital Area**
Mildred B. Hanson, President
3130 Eakin Park Court
Fairfax, VA 22031
(703)208-4253

The American-Scandinavian Foundation
of Los Angeles
Reuben Perttula, President
4613 La Marade
Bakersfield, CA 93309
(805)324-3294 (day)
(805)323-0935 (evening)

The American Scandinavian Foundation of Monterey
Harold Englund, President
20180 Portola Drive
Salinas, CA 93908
(213)455-2069

American-Scandinavian Foundation, San Francisco Bay Area
Associates
Douglas J. Tubb, President
515 Winslow Street
Crockett, CA 94525
(415)787-2356

The American-Scandinavian Foundation, Santa Barbara
Julia Rexfors, President
4141-A Via Andorra
Santa Barbara, CA 93110
(805)822-9227

American-Scandinavian Foundation/Thousand Oaks
Dr. Howard Rockstad, President
1227 Tierra Drive
Thousand Oaks, CA 91360
(805)495-7274

The Boston Associates of the American-Scandinavian
Foundation
John Gregg, President
84 Long Avenue
Belmont, MA 02178
(617)484-5748

Decorah Associates of the American-Scandinavian Foundation
Barbara Bahe, President
510 Mound Street
Decorah, IA 52101
(319)382-3992

◆ **Des Moines Associates of the American-Scandinavian Foundation**
Mrs. Blanche Peterson, President
2709 Arthur
Des Moines, IA 50317
(515)266-3482

Detroit Associates of the American-Scandinavian Foundation
Mr. Stuart Saari
31801 W. Chicago
Livonia, MI 48150
(313)533-8612 (Consul Harri Virjo)

Minnesota Associates of the American-Scandinavian Foundation
Einar O. Johnson, President
1283 Black Oak Court
Plymouth, MN 55447
(612)476-4826

◆ **Northwest Iowa Associates of the American-Scandinavian Foundation**
Ione Johnson, Corresponding Secretary
Box 154
Peterson, IA 51047
(712)295-7851

Oregon/Southwest Washington Associates of the American-Scandinavian Foundation
G. Bernhard Fedde, President
1919 N.W. Ramsey Crest
Portland, OR 97229-4209
(503)292-6503

Southern Florida Associates of the American-Scandinavian Foundation Inc.
Helen Meyer, President
8305 Sunrise Lakes Blvd., #39-108
Sunrise, FL 33322
(305)742-8067

◆ **Western Carolinas Associates of the American-Scandinavian Foundation**
Eiler R. Cook, President
PO Box 188
Etowah, NC 28729
(704)692-0323

American-Scandinavian Foundation, Santa Barbara

c/o Julia Rexfors
4141-A Via Andorra
Santa Barbara, CA 93110
Tel. (805)683-4641

President   Julia Rexfors

Founded   1951

Members   150 families

Purpose   American Scandinavian Foundation, Santa Barbara, is a diverse group interested in Scandinavian culture and lifestyle. ASF is a publicly supported, non-profit organization which promotes international understanding between the United States and Scandinavia.

Activities   Provides scholarship help for students involved in Scandinavian study or exchange at both the college and high school level. Annual events include an annual meeting; a kickoff to welcome new members in September; a Christmas dinner/dance and St. Lucia fest; the annual June Scandinavian Midsummer festival at Oak Park. Some other activities have been: a visit to a Santa Ynez winery and Iceland pony ranch; a Solvang dinner-theater evening; a trip to the San Pedro Norwegian and Swedish Seamans Home; a program at Elverhaj Museum in Solvang.

Publication   A newsletter.

◆ American Scandinavian Heritage Foundation

c/o Roland A. Swanson, Treasurer
PO Box 622
Jamestown, NY 14702-0622
Tel. (716)665-5969

President   Gerald E.C. Heglund

Founded   1966, incorporated 1983

Members   220

Purpose   The Foundation seeks to promote and advance the intellectual relations between the United States and the Scandinavian countries; to strengthen the bonds between the residents of Scandinavian descent, and all people with an interest in Scandinavia.

Activities   The organization meets eleven to twelve times per year and has planned and presented programs such as: Midsommar Frukost, Scandinavian Day at Chautauqua Institution, St. Lucia-Fest, Iceland-Finland Night, and Norwegian-Danish Night.

Publications A newsletter. SAGA FROM THE HILLS by M. Lorimor Moe (a book about the Swedes of Jamestown).

Subsidiary Group
Raoul Wallenberg Committee
c/o Mrs. Norma Anderson
RD #2, Palm Road
Jamestown, NY 14701

American Scandinavian Society, Inc.

Mari-Louise Forsgren Hedlund
245 East 49th Street
New York, NY 10017
Tel. (212)751-0714

President   Mari-Louise Forsgren Hedlund

Founded   1908

Members   Approximately 750

Purpose   The goal of the Society is to present its members and the general public with an ongoing insight into Scandinavian culture. From its inception, it has encouraged dynamic exchange with the Nordic countries in a broad range of creative and intellectual fields.

Activities   Concerts and recitals; film showings; readings; storytelling; lectures; exhibits; tours and outings; fashion shows; and a Christmas ball.

Publication SCANDINAVIAN CONTACT, a newsletter.

American Scandinavian Foundation of Monterey

c/o Violet Beahan
PO Box 1081
Monterey, CA 93942
Tel. (408)624-2838

President   Dr. Harold Englund

Founded   1970

Members   100

Purpose   To promote the cultural heritage of the Scandinavian countries; to provide programs concerning Scandinavians, and of interest to its members; to encourage interchange of persons and ideas with the Scandinavian countries; to provide social activities of interest to its members.

Activities   Showing of the movie *Letter From America*; Gerda Sundaberg, a member, talked on Queen Margrethe II of Denmark, and the celebration of her 50th birthday in 1991; Siri Eliason, Swedish Consul General from San Francisco, spoke on the American-Scandinavian Foundation, and activities of her office.

Publication   A monthly newsletter.

◆ The American Society of Swedish Engineers

5 E. 48th Street
New York, NY 10017-0005
Tel. (212)308-9580 (Sten Sture Nordine)

President   Erik Mortensen

Founded   1888

Members   210

Purpose   The purpose of the Society is the promotion of the arts and sciences connected with engineering and mechanical construction, and of scientific progress through reading, discussions, and seminars.

Activities   The Society holds an annual meeting in January and four to six technical meetings by experts in various fields, usually combined with dinner. It sponsors one or two plant visits and one or two dinner dances per year.

Publication   Occasional publication of the Society bulletin with technical articles on a specific subject.

American Swedish Cultural Foundation, Inc.

c/o Audrey Landquist
4505 N. Abbott Avenue
Minneapolis, MN 55422
Tel. (612)537-6330

Executive Director   Iner J. Johnson

Founded   1969

Purpose   To preserve the culture and heritage of Sweden by promoting programs of various types for a wide variety of listeners; to give out information on John Hanson - his political activities and achievements.

Activities   Over 100 presentations of the John Hanson Award for Excellence in Public Service have been given to people in both the United States and Sweden. Several Viking Pride Awards and Raoul Wallenberg Awards have been presented. The organization has also sponsored a St. Lucia Queen from Sweden for several years.

◆ American Swedish Historical Museum

1900 Pattison Avenue
Philadelphia, PA 19145
Tel. (215)389-1776
Fax (215)389-7701

Chairman   George Orescan

Director   Ann Barton Brown

Founded   1926

Members   800

Purpose   The American Swedish Historical Museum is a private, non-profit organization whose aim is to promote better understanding of the historic and continuing influences of Swedish people on the cultural, economic, social, and political development of the United States. The Museum collects, preserves, and interprets the cultural and historical heritage of Swedish immigrants in America.

Activities   The Museum is housed in a building modeled after a
17th century Swedish manor house. Its collection represents 350
years of Swedish-American experience in fine and decorative arts,
music, industry, science, technology, and immigration history. It
provides educational programming, as well as a variety of cultural
events such as exhibits, lectures, crafts, film series, folk dancing,
language classes, and special events.

Publication   A newsletter.

The American Swedish Historical Museum was modeled after a Swedish herrgård.

◆ The American Swedish Institute

2600 Park Avenue
Minneapolis, MN 55407
Tel. (612)871-4907
Fax (612)871-8682

Director   Bruce N. Karstadt
Founded   1929
Members   7,100

Purpose   The American Swedish Institute is a private, non-profit organization whose aims are to preserve the Swedish cultural heritage brought to the United States by Swedish immigrants through the collection, preservation, interpretation of artifacts and archival material, and to promote closer cultural ties between Sweden and the United States.

Activities   The American Swedish Institute is housed in a stately mansion built at the turn of the century by Swan J. Turnblad. The museum is open every afternoon except Monday: Tuesday-Saturday 12-4 pm, Wednesday 12-8 pm, and Sunday 1-5pm. Activities include classes in the Swedish language, traditional crafts, exercise; cultural programs; lectures; films; workshops; and concerts. Traditional holiday celebrations such as St. Lucia and Midsummer are held annually. The library and archives offer genealogy and translation services. Permanent and temporary exhibits of items from the ASI's collection and traveling exhibits of Swedish and Swedish-American artists are featured regularly.

Publications The ASI publishes a newsletter, ASI POSTEN, 11 times a year, providing members with information on the museum and activities and events. VAR SÅ GOD, a Swedish cookbook and handbook; TO AMERIKA, reproductions of the ASI's Dala painting murals; and THE AMERICAN SWEDISH INSTITUTE: A LIVING HERITAGE are published by the ASI and are available in the Bokhandel, the Institute's book store.

Auxiliaries

American Swedish Institute Associates
(operate the Museum Shop)
Arline Dewall, President
16028 S. Fifth Street
Lakeland, MN 55043

American Swedish Institute Male Chorus
Douglas Peterson, President
2335 Orchard Lane
White Bear Lake, MN 55110

American Swedish Institute Male Chorus Auxiliary
Jeanne Rustad, President
1372 W. Larpenteur
Falcon Heights, MN 55113

◆   **FEST!**
(Friends Encouraging Swedish Traditions)
John Hasselberg, President
c/o American Swedish Institute
2600 Park Avenue
Minneapolis, MN 55407

Idun Guild
Laura Parker, President
4848 Edgewood Avenue
Crystal, MN 55428

Punschklubben
Allen Ost, President
5201 46th Avenue S.
Minneapolis, MN 55417

Svea Club
Maja Vinnes, President
430 Mendota Road
West St. Paul, MN 55118

Women's Club
Bernie Engdahl, President
629 Van Buren Street
Minneapolis, MN 55413

Affiliates

◆   **Agassiz Swedish Heritage Society**
Lyndon Johnson, President
901 Birch
Hallock, MN 56728

◆   **ASI Bemidji Affiliate**
Lloyd Johnson
321 Norwood Drive N.E
Bemidji, MN 56601

Dala Heritage Society
Gordon Hallstrom, President
Rt. 1
Brook Park, MN 55007

◆   **Dalsborgs Skandinaviska Förening**
Ronald Johnson, President
Box 69, Route 1
Centerville, SD 57014

Fox Valley Swedish Society
Timothy Galloway, President
310 Cowling Baly Road
Neenah, WI 54956

◆ **Kichi-Saga Swedish Club**
Helen Fosdick, President
Box 671
Lindstrom, MN 55045

North Central Iowa Svenska Klubben
Sadie Mossberg, President
1012 Sunset Drive
Gowrie, IA 50543

◆ **Svenska Vännerna, Inc.**
Kathy Lee, Secretary
PO Box 397
Sherburn, MN 56171

◆ **Swedish Cultural Heritage Society of the Red River Valley**
Dallas Young, President
414 Forest Avenue
Fargo, ND 58102

◆ **Swedish Northern Lights Society/Nordsken Förening ASI**
Helen McDowell, President
302 S.E. Fourth Street
Deer River, MN 56636

◆ **Three Crowns American Swedish Association of Bismarck-Mandan, ND**
Q.F. Paulson, President
7051 University Drive
Bismarck, ND 58504

◆ American Swedish Institute - Bemidji Affiliate

c/o Lloyd Johnson
321 Norwood Drive N.E.
Bemidji, MN 56601
Tel. (218)751-3469

President   Ardie Olson
Founded   1976
Members   124

Purpose   The Bemidji Affiliate shares the purposes and objectives
of the American Swedish Institute as stated in the acts of incorporation and the "statement of mission and purpose," insofar as these
are relevant to the local situation.

Activities   St. Lucia fest each December 13th; Midsommerfest in
June.

Publication   NORDSTJÄRNAN, a monthly newsletter.

◆ American Union of Swedish Singers (AUSS)

c/o Dan Olch
245 W. Denver Drive
Des Plaines, IL 60018
Tel. (708)298-4888

President   Kenneth R.A. Anderson

Founded   1892

Members   700

Purpose   The purpose of the American Union of Swedish Singers
is to work for the unity of Swedish choruses and quartets with
particular emphasis on the use of Swedish and Scandinavian music
and language.

Activities   There are AUSS conventions every two years with a four
year cycle between Division conventions. Alternate two year sched-
ules of Division conventions are held regionally; i.e. Eastern, Central, and Western.

Publication   MUSIKTIDNING, a magazine published 10 times a year,
Dan Olch, Editor.

Active Choruses in AUSS

Eastern Division

Apollo Singing Society - Contact: Carl-Erik Westberg, 32
Greenhill Road, Hamden, CT 06514

Eastern Division Swedish Veterans - Contact: Phil Anderson,
334 Maple Street, East Longmeadow, MA 01028

Eastern Division Swedish Women's Chorus - Contact: Annetta
Anderson, 334 Maple Street, East Longmeadow, MA 01028

Nordic Glee Club - Contact: Esther Lundquist, 66 Croton
Avenue, Apt. 37, Ossining, NY 10562

North Star Singers - Contact: Eric L. Haffling, 264 Freeman Avenue, Stratford, CT 06497

Northern Lights Ladies' Chorus - Contact: Virginia Dorne, 51 Dudley Drive, Fairfield, CT 06430

Orphei Drängar Male Chorus - Contact: Phil Anderson, 334 Maple Street, East Longmeadow, MA 01028

Scandia Women Singers - Contact: Annetta Anderson, 334 Maple Street, East Longmeadow, MA 01028

Scandinavian Ladies' Chorus of Rhode Island - Contact: Marian Bird, 6 Wilshire Way, Coventry, RI 02816

Scandinavian Women's Chorus of Connecticut - Contact: Marijke Westberg, 32A Pilgrim's Harbor, Wallingford, CT 06492

Verdandi Male Chorus - Contact: Lennart Eliason, Widow Sweets Road, Exeter, RI 02822

Viking Male Chorus - Contact: Howard Lundgren, 45 Willow Avenue, Jamestown, NY 14701

Central Division

American Swedish Institute Male Chorus - Contact: J. Steven Swanson, 186 George Street, Excelsior, MN 55331

Arpi Male Chorus - Contact: Nils Nilsson, 9126 Beatrice, Livonia, MI 48010

Chicago Swedish Glee Club - Contact: James F. Olson, 2078 Charter Point Drive, Arlington Heights, IL 60004

Chicago Swedish Male Chorus - Contact: Robert Voedisch, 722 Haddow Street, Arlington Heights, IL 60004

Chicagoland Swedish Veterans - Contact: Alf Lundquist, 8540 N. Mansfield Avenue, Morton Grove, IL 60053

Norden Singers - Contact: Robert Dickey, 2681 Grandview, Des Moines, IA 50317

Rockford Swedish Veterans - Contact: Bertil Peterson, 6316 Park Ridge Road, Rockford, IL 61111

St. Paul Swedish Male Chorus - Contact: Henry Swanson, 1451 Hazel Street, St. Paul, MN 55119

Scandia Women's Chorus - Contact: June Jones, 18793 Elkhart, Harper Woods, MI 48225

Sveas Söner Singing Society - Contact: Carl E. Carlson, 2530 15th Avenue, Rockford, IL 61108

Suncoast Swedish Veterans - Contact: Harry Gullborg, 1011 Imperial Palm Drive, Largo, FL 33541

Waukegan Swedish Glee Club - Contact: Vince Johnson, 415 Westmoreland, Waukegan, IL 60085

Western Division

Bellman Male Chorus - Contact: William Dale, 7640 Goodlad Street, Burnaby, BC V5E 2H6 Canada

Scandia Ladies' Chorus - Contact: Jody Jones, Rt. 1, Box 197, Hillsboro, OR 97124

Scandinavian Male Chorus - Contact: David MacMillan, 3915 S.E. Crystal Springs Boulevard, Portland, OR 97202

Seattle Swedish Women's Chorus - Contact: Lilly Moen, 7514 19th Avenue N.W., Seattle, WA 98117

Svea Male Chorus - Contact: Paul Safstrom, 3425 25th Avenue W., Seattle, WA 98199

◆ Augustana Historical Society

c/o Augustana College
Rock Island, IL 61201
Tel. (309)794-7266

President   Dr. Melbert Peterson

Founded   1930

Members   202 families

Purpose   The purpose of the Society is to collect and preserve documents, publications, correspondence, and objects of historical interest relating to Scandinavians in America and the religious movements among them, especially the Augustana Lutheran Church and the Lutheran Church in general. The Society also assembles archival material and encourages historical research and publication.

Publications The Society publishes a series of historical publications. To date 39 volumes have been published on a variety of subjects.

◆ Bishop Hill Heritage Association (BHHA)

c/o Morris Nelson
PO Box 1853
Bishop Hill, IL 61419
Tel. (309)927-3513

President   Maggi Lunde

Founded   1962

Members   800

Purpose   The purpose of the Bishop Hill Heritage Association is to preserve buildings, artifacts, and documents from the colony and interpret these to the public. The Bishop Hill Heritage Association owns six Bishop Hill Colony buildings, which are restored and preserved. These buildings are used as a museum, apartment, craft production, and sales center. The Bishop Hill Heritage collection is an archives open by appointment to scholars and families doing research.

Activities   Historical preservation; managing the museum and archives; craft demonstrations; museum gift shop featuring Swedish imports and handmade crafts.

Publications A bimonthly newsletter. GUIDEBOOK TO BISHOP HILL BUILDINGS; BISHOP HILL COOKBOOK; WESTERN ILLINOIS REGIONAL STUDIES.

◆ The Cadillac Area Scandinavian Society

PO Box 958
Cadillac, MI 49601
Tel. (616)779-0823 (John Nelson)

President   John Nelson

Founded   1979

Members   150

Purpose   To foster and preserve the cultural heritage of the Scandinavian countries; to educate the general public about these customs and practices; to provide fellowship among those who are dedicated to the preservation of these ethnic values.

Activities   A St. Lucia festival; smörgåsbord; Midsummer fest; Sister City relationships; leadership in the Viking Color Festival; sponsorship of a concert and a food booth at the Cadillac Council of the Arts art festival.

Publication   NORDIC HORN, a newsletter.

◆ Carl Sandburg Historic Site Association of Galesburg

c/o Rita Carlson
PO Box 364
Wataga, IL 61488
Tel. (309)375-6392

President   Rita Carlson

Founded   January 1986

Members   16

Purpose   The purpose of the Association is to better coordinate between the State, Site Curator, and City Tourism Committee.

Activities   Monthly meetings; cultural events such as a story teller and songs; festival to promote attendance at the birthplace; a Midsummer celebration with an outside band concert is held on the Sunday closest to June 21st.

◆ The Central Swedish Committee of Chicago

c/o Carl E. Carlson
2530 15th Avenue
Rockford, IL 61108-5704
Tel. (815)397-0767

President   Carl E. Carlson

Founded   1960 (incorporated February 3, 1971)

Members   63 organizations

Purpose   The Central Swedish Committee coordinates the activities of Swedish clubs, groups, and societies in the Chicago area in their efforts to preserve Swedish culture in America.

Activities   A program at the Carl Von Linné statue in May; a
program at North Park College to commemorate Swedish Flag Day
on the first Sunday in June; in the fall, a Swedish Festival at the
Chicago Botanic Garden with displays from Swedish organizations
and a program; a St. Lucia program at Chicago's Civic Center, where
Chicago's Queen of Light is chosen from the various Swedish-
American groups. The Committee also works in cooperation with
the Swedish Consulate General serving whenever possible, especially when Swedish dignitaries visit the Chicago area.

Publication   A calendar of events listing Swedish activities in the
Chicago and Rockford areas.

Member Groups

American Daughters of Sweden
American Friends of the Emigrant Institute of Sweden
American Scandinavian Association
American Union of Swedish Singers
Bishop Hill Heritage Association
Club Dalarna
Covenant Home
Ebenezer Lutheran Church
Erickson's Delicatessen
Förgät-Mig-Ej Children's Club, Vasa Order of America
Grand Lodge, Independent Order of Svithiod
Grand Lodge, Independent Order of Vikings
Harald Lodge #13, Independent Order of Vikings
Illinois Chapter 2, Independent Order of Good Templars
Illinois District Lodge #8, Vasa Order of America
Irving Park Lutheran Church
Jupiter Lodge, Independent Order of Good Templars
Kronan Lodge #179, Vasa Order of America
Linnea - South Suburban Swedish Women's Group
Carl & Helen Madsen
Nelson World Travel
Nordic Folk Dancers of Chicago
Norrlänningarna
North Park College
North Park Seminary
Ricardo Nelson Travel Bureau
Rockford Swedish Cultural Society
Scandinavian Airlines System
Scandinavian Boutique
Scandinavian Day
Scandinavian Fraternity of America, District 6
Siljan-Mora, Tuna Lodge #134, Vasa Order of America

Skåne Club
Solstrålens Children's Club, Vasa Order of America
South Side Värmland's Klubb
SVEA
SVEA Restaurants I, II
Svenska Gillet
Svenska Kristna Föreningen
Sverige Barnen, Independent Order of Svithiod
Sweden Shop
Swedish American Athletic Association
Swedish-American Chamber of Commerce/Chicago
Swedish-American Historical Society
Swedish American Museum Center of Chicago
Swedish American Recreation Club
Swedish American Tribune
Swedish Club Foundation
Swedish Consulate
Swedish Covenant Hospital
Swedish Cultural Society
Swedish Day Committee, Independent Order of Good Templars
Swedish Engineers' Society
Swedish Gymnastic Club
Swedish Historical Society of Rockford
Swedish Retirement Association
Vårblommans Children's Club, Vasa Order of America
Verdandi Lodge #3, Independent Order of Svithiod
Vestgöta Gille
Viking Athletic Association
Viking Ship Restoration
Wikströms Catering & Deli

Dala Heritage Society

c/o Maree Nordenstrom, Secretary
973 E. Maple
Mora, MN 55051
Tel. (612)679-3794

President   Gordon Hallstrom

Founded   1977

Members   125

Purpose   The Dala Heritage Society shares the purposes and
objectives of the American Swedish Institute of Minneapolis.

Activities   Midsummer celebration and raising of Majstång; conduct the St. Lucia pageant in December; present a King Vasa Day program the day preceding the Mora, Minnesota, Vasaloppet; help sponsor the Dala Folk Dancers; support and house Swedish visitors in the community.

Publication   A quarterly newsletter.

Affiliation
American Swedish Institute
2600 Park Avenue
Minneapolis, MN 55407

◆ Dalesburg Scandinavian Association

Dalsborgs Skandinaviska Förening
Box 243, Route 1
Vermillion, SD 57069
Tel. (605)253-2575

President   Ronald A. Johnson

Founded   1977

Members   92

Purpose   To promote an interest in Scandinavia and Scandinavian-America.

Activities   Lectures; concerts; a Pea Soup and Pancake Supper; St. Lucia Festival; Annual Meeting; Scandinavian Travelers Night; Scandinavian show and taste; a Midsummer Festival. Meetings are held throughout the year.

Publications DALESBURG'S NEWS, a newsletter. HISTORY OF THE SWEDES WHO SETTLED IN CLAY COUNTY, SOUTH DAKOTA AND THEIR BIOGRAPHIES by August Peterson (1947). Slide presentation on history of Swedes in Clay County, South Dakota.

Decorah Associates of the American-Scandinavian Foundation

c/o Barbara Bahe
510 Mound Street
Decorah, IA 52101
Tel. (319)382-3992

President   Barbara Bahe

Founded   1983

Members   70-75

Purpose   The Decorah Associates of the ASF are interested in the advancement of cultural relations between the United States and the five Scandinavian countries— Denmark, Finland, Iceland, Norway, and Sweden—and in the strengthening of the bonds of friendship and international understanding between Americans and Scandinavians. This is accomplished by promoting Scandinavian culture in the community and by sponsoring a variety of cultural programs and social events.

Raising the maypole at a Midsummer Fest sponsored by the Decorah Associates of the A.S.F.

Activities   Two joint dinners and programs with the Decorah chapter of Norsemen Federation; St. Lucia program and breakfast given by the Scandinavian students at Luther College; an annual Midsommarnatt fest with a maypole, bonfire, dancing, flowers, a smörgåsbord and good fellowship; joint sponsorship of welcoming potluck supper for the Scandinavian educators attending a four week Institute in American Studies at Luther College.

Publication   President's newsletter prior to each meeting.

◆ The Delaware Swedish Colonial Society

c/o R. G. Holdway, Treasurer
4635 Griffin Drive
Wilmington, DE 19808
Tel. (302)998-9903

President   Sigurd Swensson

Founded   1937

Members   290

Purpose   To collect, preserve and publish records,documents, and other material relating to the history of Swedish settlements in America. Also, to promote understanding and appreciation of Swedish culture and traditions among the general public, and thereby foster good relations between the peoples of the United States and Sweden. On or about March 28 of each year the Society commemorates the landing of the Swedish settlers at "The Rocks" in Fort Christina Park, Wilmington, Delaware.

Activities   An annual meeting in March; a Midsummer fest in July; a fall meeting in October; a St. Lucia celebration in December.

Publications The book, CHARLES SPRINGER'S FAMILY IN SWEDISH HISTORY, by Baldwin Maull, published in 1978. DELAWARE SWEDISH COLONIAL SOCIETY, A CHRONOLOGICAL HISTORY (1937-1990) by Ruth Swanson Crossan, published in 1991.

◆ Des Moines Associates of ASF

c/o Mrs. Doris Youngberg McCollum
2319 35th Avenue
Des Moines, IA 50310
Tel. (515)277-4044

President   Jane Ann Wedman

Founded   January 1975

Members   177

Purpose   To learn more about the five Scandinavian countries' culture and heritage. To make new friends.

Activities   Monthly meetings; St. Lucia ceremony and smörgåsbord; Midsummer day celebration and smörgåsbord; tours to Bishop Hill, IL; Lindsborg, KS; and Minneapolis, MN (American Swedish Institute).

Publication SCAN-O-GRAM, a monthly newsletter.

◆ Detroit-Swedish Council, Inc.

PO Box 23
Bloomfield Hills, MI 48303-0023
(313)641-2999

Secretary   Ingrid Berge

Founded   1963

Members   125

Purpose   The purpose of the Detroit-Swedish Council is to stimulate interest in cultural matters of Swedish origin, unite for educational purposes individuals of Swedish birth, ancestry, and others
interested in Swedish art and culture, and sponsor and conduct
meetings, concerts, symposia, and exhibits of various kinds to
expand the public's knowledge of Swedish and Swedish-American
art and culture.

Activities   The Council sponsors exhibits, concerts, and lectures of
Swedish origin and coordinates various cultural and educational
events in the Detroit area. Since 1972, the Council has awarded an
annual Carl and Olga Milles Scholarship to support needy students
of the Cranbrook Academy of Art. In 1976, to commemorate the
visit to America of Sweden's king, the Council published *They Made
a Difference*, a book highlighting the Swedish influence on
Detroit and the state of Michigan. In 1984 the Council established
the Swedish Language Endowment fund at the University of Michigan. The Council also presented a Swedish Heritage week with
numerous activities and programs inviting churches and Swedish
organizations to participate. It also cooperated with the New Sweden '88 program. In 1990, Detroit-Swedish Council assisted with the
second annual Conference of Swedish America in Dearborn, Michigan, sponsored by Swedish Council of America.

Publication   Newsletter.

Duluth Swedish Cultural Society

c/o Clifford H. Hedman
4410 Gilliat Street
Duluth, MN 55804
Tel. (218)525-3775

President   Clifford H. Hedman

Founded   1966

Members   80

Purpose   To promote the retention of our Swedish background
and customs.

Activities   Midsummer festival.

◆ FEST!

Förening Efter Skandinaviska Traditioner
(Friends Encouraging Scandinavian Traditions)
c/o American Swedish Institute
2600 Park Avenue
Minneapolis, MN 55407
Tel. (612)871-4907

President   John Hasselberg (612)827-0019

Founded   May 1986

Members   45

Purpose   A public-oriented organization presenting events dealing with contemporary Scandinavian issues. FEST's goal is to promote the Scandinavian heritage and contribute to the American Swedish Institute and the community, by introducing young adults to Scandinavian culture through programming at the American Swedish Institute.

Activities   Valborgsmässoafton bonfire party; Soppaloppet; Skördefest; monthly second Saturday educational and social events at the American Swedish Institute Kaffestuga.

Publication   A quarterly newsletter.

◆ Folklife Institute of Central Kansas

118 S. Main Street
Lindsborg, KS 67456
Tel. (913)227-2007

President   Dr. Greta Swenson

Founded   1989

Purpose   To heighten public awareness of folklife and folk art; to document the material culture and oral history of central Kansas; to collect data and publish conclusions of folklife projects completed; to provide a structure and facility for other researchers to use; and to promote involvement of other groups in documenting folklife in central Kansas.

Activities   Documentation, preservation, and presentation of folklife.

◆ Friends of Scandinavia

c/o Maury Gifford
PO Box 51129
Raleigh, NC 27609
Tel. (919)878-4558

President   Maury Gifford

Founded   1979

Members   160

Purpose   To foster fellowship and friendship among the Scandinavians and others interested in Scandinavian culture; to provide
activities and programs that broaden knowledge and appreciation
of Scandinavian culture; and to preserve and keep alive the traditions and heritage of Scandinavia.

Activities   Meetings are held on the third Saturday of each month
(September through June). Other activities: bus trips; cooking classes;
sponsorship of cultural activities through the Cultural Outreach
Committee; exhibits in area libraries and schools; participation in
the International Festival of Raleigh. Annual traditions include a
Christmas fair; St. Lucia pageant; Lutefisk dinner; Syttende Mai
picnic and a Midsummer celebration.

Publications SCANDIA NEWS, a monthly newsletter; an informational brochure.

◆ Gammelgården Museum

20880 Olinda Trail North
Scandia, MN 55073
Tel. (612)433-5053

Director   Lynne Moratzka

Founded   1972

Purpose   A Swedish immigrant museum with six log buildings
situated on an 11-acre park site 35 miles from Minneapolis and
enclosed with Swedish style fencing. The buildings were built
between 1856-1868 and include: Gammel Kyrka (old church), präst
hus (parsonage); immigrant house, barn, wookshed, and stuga
(cabin).

Activities   The Museum is open from mid-May to mid-October;
other tours by arrangement. Meals can be provided for tour groups
with advance arrangements. The Museum is available for concerts,
dances, and other special events. For example, Gammel Kyrka is the

scene of many weddings. In addition, a Midsummer celebration is held each June; Spelmansstämma in August; St. Lucia Fest in December.

Publication   TIDSKRIFT, a semi-annual newsletter.

Gulf Coast Scandinavian Club

c/o Inga Lisa Calissendorff
5305 Humble Road
Dickinson, TX 77539
Tel. (713)337-1991

President   Arene Gustafson

Founded   1967

Members   60

Purpose   To unite the people in Galveston County of Scandinavian ancestry to keep alive the traditions, foods, festivals, and holidays of the Scandinavian countries.

Gustavus II Adolphus Society

1628 E. Lake Street
Minneapolis, MN 55407
Tel. (612)729-9698

Chairman   Robert Carlson

Founded   1886

Members   246

Purpose   The Society is a social organization of Swedish descendants participating in Swedish activities and supportive in the preservation of the Swedish heritage to future generations.

Activities   Social gatherings; dances; summer picnics; a Midsummer fest; meetings are held twice a month.

Publication   A monthly newsletter.

Ladies Auxiliary
Ruth Rand
7225 Emerson Avenue N.
Brooklyn Center, MN 55430
(612)561-4647

◆ Heritage Institute of Ellis Island

c/o Sten Sture Nordine
19 E. 48th Street
New York, NY 10017
Tel. (212)308-9580

President   Sten Sture Nordine

Founded   1982

Purpose   A genealogical research and listing institute of all immigration to America. Restoration and preservation of the south end
of Ellis Island, the Custom House, and Castle Clinton.

Activities   Entertainment for the passengers on the ferries to Ellis
Island.

Publication   A monthly newsletter.

◆ House of Sweden

c/o Carl Elwood
711 Amiford Drive
San Diego, CA 92107
Tel. (619)222-4669

President   Patricia Gerko

Founded   1935

Members   215

Purpose   To promote Swedish culture to the people of San Diego
and to furnish a place where those of Swedish descent can meet for
social activities.

Activities   The celebration of holidays; folk dancing; and the sponsorship of visiting singing, musical, and dancing groups from
Sweden.

Hälsingarna av Minnesota

c/o Good Templar Center
2922 Cedar Avenue South
Minneapolis, MN 55407
Tel. (612)825-9917 (Alma Erikson)

Chairman   Inga Litfin (612)439-6523

Founded   1931

Members   44

Purpose   The organization was founded by immigrants from
Hälsingland. Its purpose is to bring together people from this
province for social activities and to maintain and promote Swedish
culture.

Activities   Social.

Härjedals National Förening

c/o Ordell W. Peterson, Director
60616 Wooddale Avenue S.
Edina, MN 55424
Tel. (612)922-2172
or
c/o Kathie Lindberg, Historian
Lake Hubert, MN 56459
Tel. (218)963-2467

President   Harry Pearson, Waskish, MN

Founded   1925

Members   100+

Purpose   The purpose of the organization is to bring together
people of Härjedals origin living in the United States and to strive for
good fellowship, to preserve and foster their best traits, to revive old
memories from the fatherland, and to further the knowledge of
contribution and activities of people from Härjedalen in all walks of
life. Records of birthdays and birthplaces are kept.

Activities   A day-long meeting is held annually in different towns
in Minnesota. The meeting is called "Härjedals Möte". Some of the
events on that day include: a dinner, business meeting, a program,
and a memorial service. This group also provides a display and
information table at the annual Midsummer "Svenskarnas Dag" in
Minneapolis.

Publication   A commemorative book, HÄRJEDALEN HERITAGE, published in 1991.

Independent Order of Svithiod

c/o Betty Jane Clausen, Secretary-Treasurer
5518 W. Lawrence Avenue
Chicago, IL 60630
Tel. (312)736-1191

Grand Master Henry A. Sanderson

Founded 1880

Members Approximately 2,000

Purpose This fraternal organization promotes Swedish culture and heritage through social activities.

Activities Annual spring frolic; annual Svithiod Day outing in June; pancake brunches; smörgåsbord dinners; dances, etc. at various times throughout the year.

Publication THE SVITHIOD JOURNAL

Local Lodges:

Svithiod Lodge No. 1
Wayne Nixon, Chairman
122 King Arthur Court
Palatine, IL 60067

Manhem Lodge No. 2
Edna J. Hofverberg, Chairman
1855 W. Crescent
Park Ridge, IL 60068

Verdandi Lodge No. 3
Leonard Carlson, Chairman
6127 N. Fairfield
Chicago, IL 60659

Frithiof Lodge No. 5
Jean V. White, Chairman
270 E. Third Avenue, Box 897
Clifton, IL 60927

Thor Lodge No. 11
Ruth Weiler, Chairman
2018 Euclid Avenue
Chicago Heights, IL 60411

Linden Park Lodge No. 15
Jean Narkis, Chairman
137 W. West Drive
Northlake, IL 60164

Frej Lodge No. 16
Robert Doering, Chairman
2411 10th Street
Rock Island, IL 61201

VASA Lodge No. 17
Russell Johnson, Chairman
942 Hawkinson
Galesburg, IL 61401

Andree Lodge No. 19
Robert Armstrong, Chairman
14747 S. Laramie
Oak Forest, IL 60452

Irving Park Lodge No. 20
Inez Johnson, Chairman
5515 Washington Street
Morton Grove, IL 60053

John Ericsson Lodge No. 23
Robert L. Adams, Chairman
625 Dawson
Rockford, IL 61107

Brage Lodge No. 29
Yvonne Swanson, Chairman
21741 Benedict
Chillicothe, IL 61523

Sten Sture Lodge No. 32
Melvin P. Anderson, Chairman
518 N. Second Avenue
Maywood, IL 60153

Elida-Englewood Lodge No. 54
Eyrtha Carlson, Chairman
9633 S. Maplewood Avenue
Evergreen Park, IL 60642

Corona Lodge No. 55
Isabel Osborn, Chairman
2821 Yonge Street
Rockford, IL 61103

Orion Lodge No. 64
Gerald Schubring, Chairman
2304 Algonquin Road., Apt. 11
Rolling Meadows, IL 60008

Astrid Lodge No. 65
Lisa Verzosa, Chairman
2136 N. Mobile
Chicago, IL 60639

John Morton Lodge No. 74
Wayne Egebrecht, Chairman
3407 N. Rutherford
Chicago, IL 60634

◆ Independent Order of Vikings

c/o Barbara Lou Upstrom, Executive Director
2200 E. Devon Avenue, Suite 257
Des Plaines, IL 60018
Tel. (708)298-3550

Grand Chief William F. Nelson

Founded 1890

Members 10,256

Purpose   The purpose of the group is to unite fraternally men and women of Scandinavian birth or descent and those who are legally united in marriage to members of the Order, of sound health and good moral character, between the ages of 16 and 65, for insured membership and enable them by unity and cooperation to gain moral, intellectual, and economic strength and advancement.

Activities   Annually the Grand Lodge distributes scholarships to high school seniors through its scholarship fund. It also gives five juniors a year a chance to attend the Concordia Language Village in Moorhead, Minnesota. The 46 local lodges sponsor a variety of social activities and holiday celebrations. A 100th anniversary celebration was held in June 1990.

Publication   VIKING JOURNAL - VIKINGEN

Local Lodges   For information concerning the availability of local lodges and their activities in your area, contact the executive director at the above address.

International Order of Runeberg

c/o Raili S. Scimone, Secretary
810 Wintergreen Avenue
Hamden, CT 06514
Tel. (203)397-2683

President   Edward W. Nilson

Founded   1920

Members   1900

Purpose   The Order of Runeberg was organized as a combination
of two separate groups, the Finland-Swedes Benevolent & Aid
Association of America and the Finland-Swedes Temperance Association whose original objective and purpose was to unite in a
fraternal organization men and women who spoke and understood
Swedish, were of sober and good moral character. Today, the main
objectives of the order are fraternal and social. The Order is made up
of three districts; Central, Eastern, and Western. In turn, each
district is composed of individual lodges organized within cities of
the respective districts.

Activities   An international convention (United States, Canada,
Finland) is held every four years. The three districts (Eastern,
Central, Western), also hold conventions every four years one year
prior to the international convention. Each lodge in the Order has
its own activities.

Publications LEADING STAR/LEDSTJÄRNAN, a monthly newspaper;
newsletters are distributed by local lodges.

District Lodges

Eastern District

George Nousiainen, President
266 Mountain Road
Cheshire, CT 06408

Central District

Douglas Niltunen, President
Box 82
Dollar Bay, MI 49922

Western District

Anita Nilson, President
2104 Hayes Avenue
Anaconda, MT 59711

The International Organization of Good Templars (I.O.G.T.)

c/o Ann Finsveen, Business Manager
4337 Nokomis Avenue
Minneapolis, MN 55406
Tel. (612)724-1357
(612)721-7606 (Minneapolis office)

**National
President**   George D. Ormsby

Founded   1851

Members   Approximately 2,000

Purpose   The purpose of the I.O.G.T. is to work for the liberation of the peoples of the world to a richer, freer, and more rewarding life. The organization requires as a basis for membership total abstinence from intoxicating beverages and is totally opposed to any non-medical use of all dependence-creating or habit-forming drugs.

Activities   The local lodges and chapters sponsor different social activities and holiday celebrations. In some places the I.O.G.T. also sponsors and maintains Good Templar Parks where Midsummer celebrations as well as recreational activities are held.

Publication   NATIONAL GOOD TEMPLAR

Councils and Chapters

Atlantic Seaboard Regional Council
Miriam Ormsby, Grand Secretary
712A Drayton Road
Aston, PA 19014

Central New Jersey Chapter
Flora Liddell, Secretary
16 Redcliffe Avenue, 3B
Highland Park, NJ 08904
Chapter Address: PO Box 361, Dayton, NJ 08810

California Chapter
Greta Hansson, Secretary
520 West Grove Street
Pomona, CA 91767

Central States Regional Council
Sigrid Erikson, Secretary
14206 Nallace
Riverdale, IL 60627

New England Regional Council
Mrs. Ingeborg Hallden, G.C.T.
37 Boulder Trail
Killingworth, CT 06471

Mrs. Alice M. Levine, G. Secretary-Treasurer
103 Taunton Road
Fairfield, CT 06430

Northwest Regional Council
Robert Drew, Secretary
914 E. 4th Street
St. Paul, MN 55106

Florida Fellowship of IOGT
Otto Hanson, President
205 21st Street East
Bradenton, FL 33508

Jackson Scandinavian American Society

c/o Mrs. Vivian Erickson Rittenhouse
8315 S. Jackson Road
Clarklake, MI 49234
Tel. (517)529-9831

President   Mrs. Vivian Erickson Rittenhouse

Founded   1977

Members   70

Purpose   To increase and preserve their knowledge of the Scandinavian culture, traditions, and history; to promote this to the community at large; and to encourage good fellowship among members.

Activities   A booth at Jackson's Ethnic Fair in September; a Midsummer holiday picnic; a festive meeting in either December or, more recently, in January commemorating January 13, Christmas tree plundering.

Publication   A bimonthly newsletter.

Jenny Lind Chapel Committee

c/o Albert Lestor
3847 28th Avenue
Rock Island, IL 61201

Chairman   Albert Lestor

Founded   1973

Purpose   The Committee supervises the maintenance and use of
the Jenny Lind Chapel in Andover, Illinois, as a historic site of the
mother congregation (founded in 1850) of the Augustana Lutheran
Church. The organization gathers funds for this purpose and for the
endowment of the chapel, now on the National Register of Historic
Places. The Chapel houses a museum with items dating back to the
1850s.

Activities   Religious services are held in the Chapel from late April
until late September. A Swedish högmässa is held the last Sunday in
September.

◆ Jenny Lind Club of Detroit

c/o Lillian Lagerkvist
1543 Oakridge Drive
Rochester Hills, MI 48307
Tel. (313)656-8462

President   Maurita Holland

Founded   1937

Members   90

Purpose   To unite for educational purposes individuals of Swedish birth or ancestry interested in Swedish art and culture. To
sponsor concerts, symposia, and exhibits of various kinds so that
the public may have a better knowledge of Swedish art and culture.

Activities   Concerts; St. Lucia ball; a Swedish smörgåsbord, bazaar,
and singing of Swedish holiday songs.

Publication A monthly newsletter and a yearly handbook for members.

The John Ericsson Society

c/o Kjell Lagerstrom
250 E. 63rd Street
New York, NY 10021
Tel. (212)980-9655

President   Kjell Lagerstrom

Founded   1907

Members   100

Purpose   To perpetuate and honor the memory of Captain John
Ericsson, advance the profession of engineering, and work for
cooperation between the members of his profession in all countries,
with special recognition of those branches of engineering wherein
Captain John Ericsson's principal achievements were attained. To
promote and encourage historic research concerning the life and
works of Captain John Ericsson. To gather and disseminate information concerning the history and life of John Ericsson. To gather and
preserve books, manuscripts, papers, and relics relating to the
history, life, and works of Captain John Ericsson. To mark places of
historic interest with suitable monuments and markers where such
places and locations are connected with the life of Captain Ericsson.

Activities   Each year, the Society arranges two or three luncheons/
dinners with lectures related to John Ericsson's life and work. In
addition the Society celebrates the following annual events: March
9th, Monitor Day and annual dinner; July 31st, John Ericsson
birthday at the John Ericsson statue in Battery Park; November 23rd,
dinner on date of John Ericsson arrival in the United States.

◆ Kichi-Saga Swedish Club

c/o Jerry Tuominen, Newsletter Editor
967 N. Shore Drive
Forest Lake, MN 55025-1225
Tel. (612)464-3594

President   Helen Fosdick

Founded   1974

Members   269

Purpose   To promote the Swedish heritage and culture of the
Chisago Lakes area. To promote Swedish entertainment groups
coming to the area, by providing housing and a place to perform. To
send young people to Swedish Language Village at Sjölunden. To
celebrate the typical Swedish holidays through club activities. To

provide tour guides when necessary for Swedish groups.

Activities   Promotion of Sjölunden Language Village; Dr. Ljungmark program; promotion of the Taylors Falls Interpretive Center; Lindstrom Karl Oskar Days; Midsummer day; Julgransplundring; waffle supper.

Publication   KICHI-SAGA NYHETER, a newsletter published four to five times a year.

◆ Kingsburg District Chamber of Commerce

1401 California Street
PO Box 515
Kingsburg, CA 93631
Tel. (209)897-2925

Manager   Bill Evans

Founded   Incorporated in 1908

Purpose   There is no Swedish-American organization in Kingsburg, "The Swedish Village". Promotion and activities for the San Joaquin Valley community is the responsibility of the Chamber of Commerce.

Activities   Annual Swedish festival is held on the third Saturday in May.

Kingsburg, California's water tower is done in a Swedish manner.

Publication   Swedish festival program.

◆ Kittson County Historical Society

c/o Cindy Adams
PO Box 100
Lake Bronson, MN 56734
Tel. (218)754-4100

President   Dean Youngren

Founded   1973

Members   210

Purpose   The Historical Society is dedicated to the preservation of local history and ethnic heritage. Resources are available to anyone who is interested in genealogy.

Publications Two county history books, a booklet, and biannual newsletters.

◆ Lake Regions Swedish Heritage Society

c/o Carl Bloomquist, Chairperson
503 Eighth Street
Devils Lake, ND 58301
Tel. (701)662-2761

**Planning
Committee**   Doris Greenleaf, Hyllis McDaniel, & Helen Foughty

Founded   1979

Members   40

Purpose   To preserve the Swedish heritage and culture and to learn more about modern Sweden.

Activities   Lectures; musical entertainment; and an annual Midsummer smörgåsbord.

Leif Ericson Society, International

c/o Ivar Christensen
3 Toft Woods Way
Media, PA 19063
Tel. (215)565-0619

President   Ivar Christensen

Founded   1976

Members   999

Purpose   To promote Leif's 1003 discovery of North America; to give Leif Ericson as much credit for showing the way as others have received for following it.

Activities   Celebrating Leif Ericson Day annually in various parts of the country; providing speakers.

Publication   A newsletter.

Leif Ericson Viking Ship

c/o Gene H. Martenson
PO Box S
Swarthmore, PA 19081
Tel. (215)660-4205

President   Gene H. Martenson

Founded   1989

Members   20

Purpose   To promote Leif's 1003 discovery of North America; to educate the public about the courage and skill as shipbuilders, explorers, merchants, and warriors of our ancestors.

Activities   Annual participation in Leif Ericson Day in Philadelphia every October 9th; participation in the greeting ceremonies for the Norwegian longships, *Gaia* and two others, as they travel the United States East Coast; promoting the 1003 Viking settlement in North America and the need for better environmental practices; building a new longship and participating in the New York harbor operation Sail '92 to greet the Columbus Voyager ships; lecture on Leif Ericson.

Lindsborg Swedish Folk Dancers

Box 242
Lindsborg, KS 67456
Tel. (913)227-3578 (L'Jean Swisher)

Director   L'Jean Swisher

Founded   1963

Purpose   To learn authentic Swedish folk dances; to promote and preserve the heritage of the community; to promote and sustain Swedish folk dancing through practice and performance; to act as ambassadors from Lindsborg, Kansas—"Little Sweden USA"—and to perpetuate the Swedish heritage.

Activities   The group performs for various Swedish and Scandinavian organizations in nearby communities as well as in other states and, every four years, in Sweden.

Publications A cookbook of authentic Swedish recipes and a tape and record of Swedish music by their fiddlers.

◆ The Linneas of Texas

c/o Rose Anderson
6414 Tarna Lane
Houston, TX 77074
Tel. (713)774-6055

President   Alice Dodd

Founded   1951

Members   47

Purpose   To stimulate interest and understanding in culture and background through traditional Swedish programs and activities, and to participate in educational projects.

Activities   The Linneas of Texas Swedish Centennial Endowed Scholarship at the University of Texas at Austin is awarded annually to two or three students; books are placed in public school and city libraries; celebrations for St. Lucia in December and Midsummerfest in June each year; the Handicraft group makes and donates baby blankets and sacques to LBJ Hospital nursery; they also make and donate filled Christmas stockings to the patients at LBJ Hospital; they have twelve dolls in provincial folk dresses and a lady's folk dress on permanent loan to Houston Baptist University Museum of America Architecture and Decorative Arts.

Publication   A yearbook.

Long Island Scandinavian Society

PO Box 376
Freeport, NY 11520
Tel. (516)764-9272 (Doris Schlaich)

President   Doris Schlaich

Founder   Claire M. Jay

Founded   1979

Members   85

Purpose   To plan interesting and informative monthly programs with an informal, friendly atmosphere where all Scandinavian-Americans will feel welcome.

Activities   The Society organizes lectures on the history, literature, music, and art of all the Scandinavian countries. The group encourages the preservation of daily histories and documents, and participates in Scandinavian festivals and holiday celebrations.

Publication   A newsletter.

Manhem Club, Inc.

658 Clarence Avenue
Bronx, NY 10465
Tel. (212)822-8965

President   Carl Stenstrom (212)654-5736

Founded   1924

Members   130

Purpose   To promote the social life and welfare of members and their families.

Activities   Folk dancing; Scandinavian concerts; ski and vacation trips; sponsoring a swim team, softball team, basketball team, and a bowling league; provides restaurant and catering services. The Club has contact with other groups in the New York area such as the Long Island Commodores.

Publication   Newsletter.

Associate

> **Manhem Dancers** (folk dancing)
> c/o Ruth Johnson
> 154-11 14th Avenue
> Beechhurst, NY 11357

Mary Circle
Nebo Evangelical Lutheran Church

3914 N. Menard Avenue
Chicago, IL 60634
Tel. (312)777-6660

Leader   Harriet Anderson Schmalzer

Founded   1940

Members   20

Purpose   The Circle meets on a monthly basis for Christian fellowship and to carry on the Swedish language, sing, and pray in Swedish with limited Swedish conversation.

◆ The Midwest Institute of Scandinavian Culture, Inc.

PO Box 522
Eau Claire, WI 54701
Tel. (715)834-1504 (Lawrence Wahlstrom)

President   John P. Hanson
Founded   1960
Members   350

Purpose   The Institute's purpose is to promote a better understanding and appreciation of Scandinavian culture.

Activities   Social events, classes, exhibits, lectures, and concerts. They also plan to build a Scandinavian Center on a 60-acre site in Dunn County, Wisconsin.

Publication   A quarterly newsletter.

Mississippi Svenska Kulturförbundet

PO Box 4654
Jackson, MS 39216
Tel. (601)366-2991 (Carl F. André)

President   Carl F. André
Founded   1984
Members   40

Purpose   To encourage appreciation of Swedish culture and to provide fellowship for Swedish-Americans.

Activities   Midsummer fest and St. Lucia Day as well as informal gatherings two or three times a year.

Publication   A newsletter.

◆ New Sweden Cultural Heritage Society of Oregon and Washington

c/o Ross Fogelquist
8740 S.W. Oleson Road
Portland, OR 97223
Tel. (503)244-3697

President   Ross Fogelquist
Founded   April 1989

Members   200

Purpose   The Heritage Society is a cultural and historical organization. The members hope to build a Swedish Center someday. They
also hope to write materials on the Swedish influence in Oregon and
Washington. Special programs include Midsummer, etc. The organization would like to sponsor individuals and groups from Sweden,
such as choirs, etc.

Activities   Christmas celebrations; Midsummer celebrations; Swedish pancake breakfast; antique and Swedish outdoor cafe; Scanfair;
Swedish language classes.

Publication   A newsletter published every three months.

◆ New Sweden Farmstead/Museum

c/o Dennis R. Campbell
Bridgeton/Cumberland Tourist Association
50 East Broad Street
Bridgeton, NJ 08302
Tel. (609)451-4802

President   Ann Karlsson-LeFever

Founded   April 1988

Purpose   The Farmstead/Museum was created for the operation of
a living history museum consisting of seven log cabin replicas of a
17th century Swedish farmstead.

Activities   Annual Midsummer Festival; craft events take place
throughout the year; participation in the Bridgeton open house tour
and Music and Heritage Festival.

◆ New Sweden Historical Society

c/o David G. Anderson
Timmerhuset
New Sweden, ME 04762
Tel. (207)896-3370

President   David G. Anderson

Founded   1925

Members   204

Purpose   The purpose of the Society is to preserve and promote
the history of the New Sweden Colony and to keep the Swedish
culture and heritage alive. The sons and daughters of the New

Sweden colony maintain 'kapitoleum', three floors of which illustrate immigrant history in northern Maine. Adjacent to the old capitol are the Lindsten Stuga, a restored immigrant cabin, and the capitol hill school, a one-room tin-ceilinged schoolhouse. The Lars Noak blacksmith shop is now open.

Activities   Midsummer is an annual two-day fest which offers Swedish music, dance, food, colorful wildflowers, and costumes. New Sweden Day is observed in July and additional Swedish-American activities are scheduled throughout the year.

Publication   A newsletter.

The Noble's Swedes

c/o John Vihlen
RFD I
Round Lake, MN 56167

President

Founded

Members   30-35

Purpose   To come together as Swedes and Swedish descendants.

Activities   Musical entertainment; singing Swedish songs; serving of Swedish foods; a Midsummer picnic.

◆ Noon Day Scandinavian Club

c/o I.A. "Al" Johnson
26 Ginger Cove Road
Valley, NE 68064
Tel. (402)359-2046

President   I.A. "Al" Johnson

Founded   1909

Members   147

Purpose   The Club is a patriotic and public-spirited American organization of Omaha business and professional men of Scandinavian birth or descent dedicated to public service and the promotion of acquaintance and good fellowship among its members.

Activities   A Christmas brunch especially for children; participation in the Ethnic Festival in Omaha; serving as hosts to visiting groups from Scandinavia; providing a scholarship for teenagers interested in attending the International Language Village.

Publication   A newsletter.

◆ Norden Club of Jamestown

c/o L. Durand Peterson
17 Wembley Drive, W.E.
Jamestown, NY 14701
Tel. (716)664-6880

President   Daniel G. Johanson

Founded   1911

Members   75 Active, 15 Social

Purpose   The purpose of the Club is to perpetuate the Scandinavian heritage and promote the intellectual well-being of its members.

Activities   A Christmas party; the Annual meeting; a Midsummer fest and a Harvest dinner. They also assist in the sponsoring of exchange students from Jamestown Community College to Södra Vätterbygdens Folkhögskola, Jönköping, Sweden, and also hold receptions for famous Swedish dignitaries visiting the area.

The Norden Club of Lincoln

c/o Dorothy Ekblad, Secretary/Treasurer
1330 Sycamore Drive
Lincoln, NE 68510
Tel. (402)488-6018

Presidents   Stuart and Martha Maseman

Founded   1947

Members   275

Purpose   To promote fellowship among individuals of Scandinavian descent; to interest the members in preserving the best in cultural heritage of Scandinavia, and to help promote progress of the nation, state, and community.

Activities   Recent activities include: Dr. Frederick Luebke discussing "Patterns of Swedish Immigration"; the showing of a film depicting life and activities on the Faroe Islands; breakfast with Anders Thunborg, the Swedish ambassador to the United States.

Publication   A quarterly newsletter.

◆ Norden Women's Club

c/o Mrs. J. Emerson Weaver
16 Engelwood Avenue
Jamestown, NY 14701
Tel. (716)487-3413

President   Mary Lou Westrom

Founded   1916

Members   100

Purpose   To promote interest in things Scandinavian and to preserve the traditions, customs, and folklore of Scandinavian people. To preserve records, documents, and historical items.

Activities   Swedish exchange program information; contributions to the American Swedish Historical Foundation/Museum; tracing of Swedish heritage.

Publication A yearbook.

The Nordic Folk Dancers of Chicago

c/o Anita Olson, Business Manager
737 S. Jackson
Hinsdale, IL 60521
Tel. (312)828-3746

President   Tim Eischen

**Dance
Instructor**   Linnea Johnson

Founded   1973

Members   22

Purpose   The organization promotes Scandinavian culture through the instruction, practice, and presentation of authentic Scandinavian folk dances and music for the education of club members, as well as the general public.

Activities   In addition to folk dance activities, the group also arranges workshops with visiting Scandinavian groups and individuals.

◆ Nordic Heritage Museum

3014 N.W. 67th Street
Seattle, WA 98117
Tel. (206)789-5707

Director   Marianne Forssblad
Founded   1979
Members   2,200
Purpose   The purpose of the Museum is to collect, document,
preserve, and exhibit artifacts, books, and archival materials relating
to those settlers and descendants of settlers who came from each of
the five Nordic countries. To serve as a cultural center for Scandinavian-Americans in the Pacific Northwest and to maintain cultural
ties through exchange of exhibits with the Nordic countries.

Activities   Exhibits; language and crafts center; regular classes in
the Nordic languages and Nordic crafts; fairs and special events;
concerts; lectures and film series.

Publications A newsletter and exhibit catalogs.

Nordic Women's Cultural Club of Texas

c/o Agnete Vaughan
12525 Broken Baugh
Houston, TX 77024

President   Agnete Vaughan
Founded   1983
Members   100
Purpose   To maintain a close contact between women from the
five Nordic countries and to promote knowledge and understanding
of historical, cultural, and current issues, both in the United States
and the Scandinavian countries.

Norsk Høstfest Association

c/o Pamela Alme Davy
PO Box 2111
Minot, ND 58702
Tel. (701)852-2368

President   Chester M. Reiten

Founded   1978

Purpose   The Norsk Høstfest is a five-day fall festival to promote the Scandinavian heritage. The Høstfest attracts over 60,000 people annually.

Activities   Entertainers from America and Scandinavia perform, craftsmen are invited to participate, and a wide variety of ethnic foods is available. The Hall of Fame banquet is held during the festival.

Publications   Two major direct mail pieces and an official program.

North Central Iowa Svenska Klubben

c/o Maynard Peterson
RR
Fonda, IA 50540
Tel. (712)468-2412 or
Gayle Pierson
RR 2
Fort Dodge, IA 50501
Tel. (515)576-6006

President   Sadie Mossberg

Founded   1976

Members   102

Purpose   To preserve the Swedish heritage, and to provide fellowship for people of Swedish heritage and similar backgrounds.

Activities   A potluck and St. Lucia program in December; a picnic each June in Kennedy Park; hosting Swedish groups such as dancers, musicians, etc.; the group meets once a month with a luncheon following the business meeting.

◆ Northwest Iowa Associates of the American-Scandinavian Foundation

c/o Ione Johnson, Corresponding Secretary
Box 154
Peterson, IA 51047
Tel. (712)295-7851

President   Robert Ohrlund

Founded   1971

Members   125

Purpose   To preserve and promote Scandinavian traditions, culture, and customs.

Activities   A St. Lucia festival; picnics in the spring and fall, and other social events.

Publication   A newsletter.

Nytta och Nöje

c/o Marion Bjornson
2113 14th Street
Rock Island, IL 61201

President   Chairman: Marion Bjornson

Founded   1900

Members   30

Purpose   The organization's purpose is to preserve the Swedish heritage and language.

Activities   The group's monthly meetings feature programs related to Swedish topics. A portion of each meeting is conducted in the Swedish language.

◆ Oakland Chamber of Commerce

Gaila Waugh, Manager
401 N. Oakland Avenue
Oakland, NE 68045
Tel. (402)685-5094

President   John M. Thomas

Members   80

Purpose   To promote actively the Oakland area for growth in population, thus increasing the need for new or expanded businesses and housing. To promote the town's Swedish heritage through tourism, and the Swedish festival.

Activities   The biennial Swedish festival, including presentations in other communities; hosting of Chautauqua '90; Swedish style show and luncheon; banquets for former Governor Kay Orr and visiting Swedish Ambassador Anders Thunborg.

Publication   A quarterly newsletter.

Oregon/Southwest Washington Associates of American-Scandinavian Foundation

c/o G. Bernhard Fedde
1919 N.W. Ramsey Crest
Portland, OR 97229-4209
Tel. (503)292-6503

President   G. Bernhard Fedde

Founded   1978

Members   110

Purpose   The organization stems from the American-Scandinavian Foundation and tends to emphasize academic ties and subjects. It tries not to duplicate work being done by the other 43 Scandinavian organizations in this area.

Activities   Lectures on Scandinavia; genealogical workshop; scholarship to take Scandinavian classes at Portland State University; concerts; booster group for Scandinavian students; hosting a Pacific Coast Regional Association of A.S.F.

Publication   A newsletter.

◆ Ozark Scandinavian Society of Springfield, Missouri (OSSSM)

c/o Karl Berglund
2050 E. Camorene
Springfield, MO 65803
Tel. (417)833-0847

President   Karl Berglund

Founded   June 1, 1987

Members   133

Purpose   To enrich the lives of the members with the charm and beauty of the Scandinavian culture and to increase interest and knowledge of our Scandinavian heritage, including Sweden, Norway, Denmark, Finland, and Iceland.

Activities   Christmas smörgåsbord with St. Lucia Fest; slide presentation by a Swedish student of Swedish nature; slide presentation of scenes from Sweden and Norway; activation of our group designating Springfield, Missouri as a Jubilee City of New Sweden '88.

Publication   OSSSM NEWS, a monthly newsletter.

Pacific Coast Regional Association of Scandinavian Organizations

c/o Ross Fogelquist
8740 S.W. Oleson Road
Portland, OR 97223
Tel. (503)244-3697

Chairman   Ross Fogelquist

Founded   1984

Members   1,200 (7 member organizations)

Purpose   To assist the Scandinavian organizations in the accomplishment of their purposes; to provide and coordinate speakers and programs on the Pacific Coast and to disseminate information concerning activities of the member organizations.

Activities   Meetings are held once or twice a year, sometimes in conjunction with a regional meeting of The American-Scandinavian Foundation of New York.

Publication   A newsletter published twice a year.

◆ Positive Sweden/North America

c/o Barbro Sachs-Osher
431 E. Strawberry Drive
Mill Valley, CA 94941
Tel. (415)388-8311
Fax (415)388-1103

President   Barbro Sachs-Osher

Founded   1990

Purpose   Positive Sweden/North America works to enhance and establish a correct and positive image of present-day Sweden through seminars, breakfast meetings, educational conferences, etc. The target groups are selected Americans, Swedes in North America, and in the near future, Swedish-Americans. Positiva Sverige in Sweden was founded in 1985 by the Employers' Organization and the Federation of Wholesalers. It has 150 members among corporations and organizations with international orientation.

Activities   Breakfast meetings with Ambassador Thunborg and Elizabeth Söderström; lunch seminars with Inez Svensson and Beate Sydhoff, all targeted towards Americans; full day education seminars to update Swedes on Sweden; cultural seminars for IKEA sales organizers.

Publications A pamphlet of educational materials for students going abroad (available in Swedish only).

Affiliate

> **Positiva Sverige**
> c/o Birgitta Wistrand
> Box 5512
> S-114 85 Stockholm
> SWEDEN
> Tel. 011 46 8 663 52 80
> Fax 011 46 8 667 80 51

◆ The Raoul Wallenberg Committee of the United States, Ltd.

245 Park Avenue, 38th floor
New York, NY 10167
Tel. (212)272-7790
Fax (212)272-9720

President   Rachel Oestreicher Haspel

Director   Susan Mesinai

Founded   May 1981

Purpose   The Committee was established to educate the public about Raoul Wallenberg, an honorary citizen of the United States whose heroic actions in Hungary during World War II are credited with saving the lives of as many as one hundred thousand persons.

Activities   An exhibit: "A Tribute to Raoul Wallenberg"; a speakers bureau; provides information packets about Raoul Wallenberg to interested students; currently developing and testing a curriculum called "Raoul Wallenberg: Heroes Curriculum" for schools and other groups such as Scouts. (Should be available in September 1992.)

Publications   A newsletter; a monograph, RAOUL WALLENBERG: A HERO FOR OUR TIME by Rachel Haspel.

Red Wing Swedish Singers

c/o Vernon Larson
1103 East Avenue
Red Wing, MN 55066
Tel. (612)388-9550

Director   Vernon S. Larson

Founded   1976

Members   52

Purpose   The chorus gives performances of both sacred and secular music, entirely in Swedish.

Activities   The Singers perform for church services, holiday celebrations, and other events.

Publication   RED WING SINGS SWEDISH 1982, a record.

St. Peter/Mankato Associates of the American Scandinavian Foundation

Gustavus Adolphus College
St. Peter, MN 56082
Tel. (507)933-7572

President   Chester Johnson

Founded   1970

Purpose   To sustain and promote the Scandinavian heritage of people in this area.

Activities   May and Yule Tide breakfast; lectures; music program; trips to places of historic interest in Scandinavian Minnesota.

◆ San Antonio Scandinavians

c/o Barbara Soule Larson
3722 Chartwell
San Antonio, TX 78230
Tel. (512)699-9311

President   Barbara Barbour
Founded   May 1978
Members   75
Purpose   To promote fellowship and stimulate interest in the history, culture, and traditions of Scandinavia.
Activities   Midsummerfest; Julfest with smörgåsbord; St. Lucia fest; movies of Scandinavia; talks on Vikings and other pertinent topics. The ladies meet monthly during the day for cooking and language lessons, crafts, etc.
Publication Bimonthly newsletter.

Scandi-American Club of Charlotte County, Florida

c/o Arla Marteliano
3033 Pellam Boulevard
Port Charlotte, FL 33948
Tel. (813)625-7310

President   Arla Marteliano
Founded   1988
Members   48
Purpose   Social enjoyment.
Activities   Slide shows.

◆ Scandinavian American Foundation of Georgia

Dennis Carlson
PO Box 1166
Decatur, GA 30031-1166
Tel. (404)377-4825

President   Dennis Carlson

Founded   March 3, 1983

Members   150

Purpose   The Foundation seeks to provide an avenue of exchange between the individual nations of Scandinavia and Georgia. Endeavors include cultural, artistic, and educational programs.

Publication   INSIGHTS, a quarterly newsletter.

Scandinavian-American Society, Inc.

7575 Crown Point
Omaha, NE 68134
Tel. (402)572-9790
(402)397-2084 (Harry Severson)

President   Astrid Olson

Founded   1975

Members   Approximately 400

Purpose   The organization is comprised of three Lodges: Orvar Odd #24, Omaha Lodge #330 (Vasa Order of America) and the Noon Day Scandinavian Club. The purpose of the organization is to provide aid and assistance to its aged, ill, or needy members, and to promote the heritage, culture, and traditions handed down by its forefathers.

Activities   The Scandinavian-American Society acts as a center for Omaha-area Scandinavian social and cultural activities, such as language classes, Midsummer festival, and an annual smörgåsbord in November.

Publication   SCANDIA, a newsletter.

Scandinavian Association of Central Florida - Hagar Viking Club

c/o Nils Gustafsson
3309 Monteen Drive
Orlando, FL 32806
Tel. (407)851-7314

President   Al Frink

Founded   1977

Members   120

Purpose   A social club that holds a monthly party, dance, or
          picnic.

Activities   A St. Lucia pageant, dinner, and dance; Swedish Night
          featuring Swedish food, live music, and entertainment; an Easter
          picnic with an Easter egg hunt for the children and games for all; a
          Midsummer celebration in June.

Publication   A monthly newsletter.

The Scandinavian Center

Dr. Nadia M. Christensen,
Executive Director
2400 Butler Place
Minneapolis, MN 55424
Tel. (612)332-0479

President   Dr. Joel S. Torstenson

Founded   1983

Members   contributing membership, ca. 350

Purpose   The Center was formed by Scandinavian-Americans in
          cooperation with Augsburg College to provide a continuing forum
          for the exchange of information and ideas about contemporary
          Scandinavia.

Activities   The Center promotes and sponsors a wide variety of
          lectures, concerts, seminars, and other events to promote an on-
          going interest in present-day Scandinavia and to nurture interculteral
          relations between the Scandinavian nations and the United States.

Publication   THE SCANDINAVIAN CENTER NEWS, a newsletter pub-
          lished five times a year.

Scandinavian Club of Albuquerque

c/o Knute Lee
13137 Montgomery Boulevard N.E.
Albuquerque, NM 87111
Tel. (505)298-5947

President   Knute Lee

Founded   1972

Members   150

Purpose   The purpose of the Club is to foster interest in Scandinavian life and culture; to spread knowledge of Scandinavian history, literature, art, traditional music, and dance by means of activities and programs; to perpetuate traditions of the Scandinavian people; and to provide for fellowship among members of the Club through meetings and social activities.

Activities   Concerts; exhibits; films; social events; holiday celebrations such as Julfest and Midsummer fest; and monthly meetings. The Club sponsors classes in language, crafts, and folk dancing. They also select, purchase, and donate books to libraries in Albuquerque.

Publications Scandinavian Club News, a newsletter. The Club has compiled a bibliography of Scandinavian subject materials for the University of New Mexico Libraries, the Albuquerque public schools, and the Albuquerque public libraries.

Affiliates   Nordic Dancers of Albuquerque, Northland Dancers (Children's group), Scandia Dancers Uff Da Band.

The Scandinavian Club of Columbus

c/o Hap Hinkle
1036 Stoney Creek Road
Columbus, OH 43235
Tel. (614)846-0210

President   Hap Hinkle

Founded   February 16, 1937

Members   120 families

Purpose   To preserve the heritage and culture of the Nordic countries of Denmark, Finland, Iceland, Norway, and Sweden.

Activities   Monthly dinner meetings with one meeting each year devoted to a Scandinavian country; participation in the Columbus International Festival; a St. Lucia festival in December; Fastelavn celebration in February; a Midsummer celebration in June; a breakfast picnic in September.

Publication   SCANDINEWS, a monthly newsletter.

◆ Scandinavian Club of Greater Kansas City

c/o Norman Danielsen
9512 Lamar
Overland Park, KS 66207
Tel. (913)381-2846

President   Norman Danielsen

Founded   1950

Members   160 (men only)

Purpose   To promote understanding of the Scandinavian cultures to the general public as well as to its members. They also sponsor scholarships for students in the United States and the Scandinavian countries.

Activities   A Christmas smörgåsbord in December; a spring meeting; a dinner and banquet in May; participation in ethnic festivals in Missouri and Kansas as well as other social activities.

Publication   SCAN-NOTES, a newsletter.

Auxiliary
Women's Auxiliary of the Scandinavian Club of Greater Kansas City
c/o Gretchen Esping-Swanson, President
4945 Neosho
Shawnee Mission, KS 66205
(913)262-9633

Scandinavian Club of Hawaii

PO Box 62001 Manoa Station
Honolulu, HI 96839-2001
Tel. (808)941-0218

President   Gunnar Danielson

Founded   1933

Members   125

Purpose   The purpose of the club is to meet on a social basis to further the spread of the cultures of the Scandinavian countries.

Activities   Midsummer Fest in June; a St. Lucia Christmas party; and quarterly meetings.

Publication   A newsletter.

Scandinavian Club, Inc.

1351 S. Pine Creek Road
Fairfield, CT 06430
Tel. (203)259-1571 or 259-3817

President   Milton Forstrom

Founded   June 3, 1916

Members   470

Purpose   To preserve the Scandinavian culture through meetings, discussions, social dances, folk dances, singing groups, etc.

Activities   Club members enjoy social activities such as dances, holiday celebrations, dinners, folk dancing, folk music, and Swedish language classes.

The Scandinavian Council of the Washington, DC Area

c/o Osten Magneheim
6101 Loch Raven Boulevard,
Suite 616
Baltimore, MD 21239-2008
Tel. (301)532-6630

President   Osten Magneheim

Founded   November 25, 1974

Members   14 member organizations

Purpose   To promote understanding and close relations between and among Scandinavians and Americans; to develop understanding and appreciation for Scandinavian customs and traditions; to promote cooperation among the Scandinavian organizations in the Washington area through joint planning and activities.

Activities   350th anniversary of New Sweden; "Salute to Scandinavia", a formal dinner dance at the World Trade Center in Baltimore.

Member Organizations

American Scandinavian Association of the National Capital Area
c/o Marilyn Benson
10 Shanandale Court
Silver Spring, MD 20904
(301)572-7270

Danish Club
c/o Helle Starcke
12732 Viers Mill Road
Rockville, MD 20853
(301)933-2313

Finlandia Foundation, Baltimore Chapter
c/o Kalevi Olkio
5101 Holder Avenue
Baltimore, MD 21214
(301)276-1311

Finlandia Foundation, National Capital Chapter
c/o Patricia Coulter
215 A Street N.E.
Washington, DC 20002
(202)543-5249

Icelandic Association
c/o Heida Kristjansdottir
6149 Summer Park Drive
Alexandria, VA 22310
(703)719-0627

Kipina Kerho
c/o Helena Elwood
11705 Basswood Drive
Laurel, MD 20708
(301)470-3470

Nordic Dancers
c/o Lars Johanson
2303 Eagle Rock Place
Silver Spring, MD 20906
(301)871-8153

Norwegian American Club of Maryland
c/o Robert Jones
6816 Blenheim
Baltimore, MD 21212
(301)377-8663

Norwegian Society of Washington, DC
c/o Gunnar Grotos
The Grove Rt 1, Box 63
Delaplane, VA 22025
(703)364-4202

Sons of Norway, Nordkap Lodge #215
c/o Aud-Sonja Sorteberg
1 Carriage Walk Court
Baltimore, MD 21234
(301)661-2750

Sons of Norway, Washington Lodge #428
c/o Barbara Westby
7700 Westfield Drive
Bethesda, MD 20817
(301)320-5395

◆   **Svea, Washington, DC**
c/o Anna Dahlberg
3541 S. Utah Street
Arlington, VA 22206

◆   **Sveaborg Society of Baltimore, Maryland**
c/o Osten Magneheim
6101 Loch Raven Boulevard
Baltimore, MD 21239
(301)532-6630

◆   **Vasa Order of America, Drott Lodge #168**
c/o Ron Carlson
616 Putnam Place
Alexandria, VA 22302
(703)549-5908

◆ Scandinavian Cultural Council of Pacific Lutheran University

Scandinavian Cultural Center
Pacific Lutheran University
Tacoma, WA 98447
Tel. (206)535-8797 Fax (206)535-8320

President   Earl Hildahl

Founded   1978

Members   26

Purpose   The Scandinavian Cultural Council brings together individuals and ethnic organizations of the Pacific Northwest to preserve the heritage and culture of the Nordic countries, to promote understanding of the immigrant experience, to strengthen ties with contemporary Scandinavia, and to support Pacific Lutheran University's Scandinavian Studies Program.

Activities   In addition to monthly meetings, the Council sponsors programs such as Nordic Night, St. Lucia festival, Norwegian Christmas service, Finnish and Icelandic Christmas festivities, Danish Fastelavn, as well as musical concerts, lectures, arts and craft classes and demonstrations, cooking classes, and language classes. A variety of exciting exhibits are on display in the three major exhibit areas located in the Center.

Publication   SCANDINAVIAN SCENE, a bimonthly newsletter.

◆ Scandinavian Cultural Society of Greater Hartford

c/o Holger Lundin
34 Main Street
Terryville, CT 06786
Tel. (203)589-8666

President   Holger Lundin

Founded   1980

Members   250

Purpose   To publicize and promote the study and preservation of the heritage and cultural values that derive from the five Scandinavian countries, Denmark, Finland, Iceland, Norway, and Sweden.

Activities   They have speakers, lectures, music, slides, folk dancing, and craft presentations from the five Scandinavian countries.

Publications A newsletter; NORDIC LEGACY, a fifth anniversary booklet.

Scandinavian Folkdancers of Raleigh

c/o Ruth Allinger
1920 Hillock Drive
Raleigh, NC 27612
Tel. (919)787-2505

Instructors   John and Ruth Allinger

Founded   1981

Members   20

Purpose   The group performs folk dances from the Scandinavian countries as a means of educating and developing an appreciation for the Scandinavian countries and to increase pride in fulfillment of one's own heritage.

Activities   The group performs throughout the state of North Carolina at various festivals and events. They are willing to negotiate performances in the Eastern part of the country.

◆ Scandinavian Heritage Group

c/o Doris Craig
HCO1 Box 99
Maxwell, NE 69151
Tel. (308)582-4486

President   Marilyn Ristine

Founded   1976

Members   225

Purpose   The group includes anyone with Scandinavian heritage in the Gothenburg/North Platte, Nebraska area. As the United States becomes more homogeneous, they feel it is important, as well as enjoyable, to preserve their rich Scandinavian heritage, culture, and customs.

Activities   St. Lucia fest in December; Midsummer fest in June; a spring smörgåsbord; a fall smörgåsbord. They sponsor a booth at the Nebraskaland Days ethnic day in North Platte, and in September at the Gothenburg Harvest Festival. They sponsor a Swedish dance group composed of mostly junior and senior high school age young people; they give two or more scholarships to Concordia Language Village in Minnesota each year.

Scandinavian Heritage Society of Kentucky

c/o Marie L. Hosie
1644 Donelwal Drive
Lexington, KY 40511
Tel. (606)252-7915

President   Kenneth Hanson

Founded   1978

Members   100

Purpose   To preserve and promote the culture and heritage of the Scandinavian countries. The Society is open to people who are of Scandinavian descent and to those who are interested in the Scandinavian culture.

Activities   A literary group that meets to discuss Scandinavian literature; a St. Lucia festival; pea soup dinner; 17th of May celebration; a Midsummer celebration; an annual founders' banquet in October; an annual meeting and smörgåsbord in March.

Publication   FINDS, a newsletter.

The Scandinavian Society of Cincinnati

c/o Ruth Ullberg
6532 Park Lane
Cincinnati, OH 45227
Tel. (513)271-3076

President   Jorgen Jorgenses

Founded   1963

Members   250 plus

Purpose   The Scandinavian Society is an incorporated, non-profit organization of native Scandinavians, people with Scandinavian ancestors, and those with interest in Scandinavia who work to promote interest in, and appreciation of, Scandinavian traditions and culture.

Activities   Regular dinner meetings and picnics to celebrate the traditional holidays and events; participating in the annual International Folk Festival; supporting international student exchanges; participating in various charitable activities including making contributions to the Cincinnati Public Library for the purchase of books on Scandinavia and assisting C.C.M. Scandinavian students.

Publication   A newsletter.

◆ Scandinavian Society of Greater Lansing

c/o K. Kenneth Forsman
11400 Dimondale Highway
Dimondale, MI 48821
Tel. (517)646-8030

President   Eleanor Renfrew

Founded   1977

Members   177 voting members and 28 associate members

Purpose   To further the knowledge, understanding, and traditions of the Scandinavian culture, and to promote fellowship among members in the community.

Activities   The Society promotes its cultural, educational, and social activities through meetings, classes, lectures, fund raising, and holiday celebrations. The Society also contributes to local libraries and provides scholarship assistance.

Publication   A newsletter.

◆ Scandinavian Society of Wichita

PO Box 48291
Wichita, KS 67201-8291

President   Bertil Van Boer

Founded   1937

Members   155

Purpose   To promote the spirit of good fellowship among those members of the community interested in Scandinavia and its culture, both past and present.

Publications   Cookbooks entitled SIMPLY SCANDINAVIAN and SUPERBLY SCANDINAVIAN.

◆ Scandinavian Studies Department, University of Minnesota

Diane Berube, Executive Secretary
200 Folwell Hall
9 Pleasant Street S.E.
Minneapolis, MN 55455-0124
Tel. (612)625-9887

Chairperson Professor Jack Zipes

Founded March 2, 1883

Purpose An academic university department of Scandinavian languages and literature.

Activities Sponsor speakers (Nordic Round Table).

Publications NORDIC BULLETIN, a monthly newsletter published October through June. A book series, Nordic Roundtable Papers.

Scandinavian Summerfest

Katherine Liden
1515 Los Arboles
Albuquerque, NM 87107
Tel. (505)344-6330

Coordinator Katherine Liden

Founded 1983

Purpose The Scandinavian Summerfest is a celebration held in the Civic Plaza in downtown Albuquerque. It is a cooperative effort of Scandinavian groups in the Albuquerque area.

Activities Some of the activities during this celebration include: arts and crafts booths; performances by local Scandinavian dance groups and musicians as well as groups from other parts of the United States and Scandinavia; Scandinavian story telling of folk tales; a fiddlers' procession and dancing around the maypole.

Smålands Förbundet

c/o Arlene L. Gross, Vice President
4446 Cedar Lake Road, #4
St. Louis Park, MN 55416
Tel. (612)377-2063

President Kenneth Haag

Founded   1932

Members   75

Purpose   The organization's purpose is to provide a place for people from the province of Småland to meet and socialize and to sustain their Swedish customs and culture.

Activities   Social activities such as speakers, slides, music, smörgåsbords, and a special Christmas fest.

Society for the Advancement of Scandinavian Study

c/o Janet Rasmussen, Vice President for Academic Affairs
Nebraska Wesleyan University
5000 Saint Paul Avenue
Lincoln, NE 68504-2796

President   Janet Rasmussen

Founded   1910

Members   600

Purpose   The Society's purpose is the promotion of Scandinavian study and instruction; the encouragement of original research in the fields of Scandinavian language, literature, history, government, and society, and the provision of a medium for the publication of the results of such research; the fostering of closer relations between persons interested in Scandinavian studies in America and elsewhere.

Activities   Annual conference.

Publications SASS NEWS AND NOTES, a newsletter, and SCANDINAVIAN STUDIES, a quarterly journal.

Society Åland

c/o Karin L. Wennström
51 Holmes Avenue
Hartsdale, NY 10530

President   Karin L. Wennström

Founded   1914

Members   90

Purpose   Originally an active sports club, the Society today provides members with sick and funeral benefits.

Activities   The Society's activities include social events and holiday
celebrations.

South Side Värmlands Klubb

c/o Wilbur Johnson
3640 West 85th Street
Chicago, IL 60652
Tel. (312)582-5614

President   Wilbur Johnson

Founded   1948

Members   200

Purpose   To unite people of Swedish descent and their families to
their common advantage and benefit.

Activities   Annual dinners, bake sale, Christmas party for children,
and Swedish dances at most meetings.

The Southern Florida Associates of the American-Scandinavian Foundation

c/o Helen U. Meyer
8305 Sunrise Lakes Boulevard
Sunrise, FL 33322
Tel. (305)742-8067

President   Helen U. Meyer

Founded   1962

Members   50

Purpose   To promote cultural exchange between the United States
and the five Scandinavian countries.

Activities   A Christmas dinner; a Spring luncheon; monthly meetings are held November through April.

◆ Stockholm Historical Society

c/o Axel Tall
Stockholm, ME 04783
Tel. (207)896-5283

President   Axel Tall

Founded   1976

Members   100

Purpose   The purpose of the Society is to maintain a historical museum which houses artifacts and documents from the time of the first pioneers to the area.

Activities   Some of the activities of the Society are to collect, identify, preserve, and display historical objects.

Publication   A newsletter.

◆ SVEA of Chicago

c/o Harriet Genberg, Newsletter Editor
833 S. Harvard Drive
Palatine, IL 60067
Tel. (708)359-8411

President   Charlotta Anton

Founded   1981

Members   200

Purpose   To keep in touch with Sweden of today and with Swedes in the area. To preserve the Swedish language and traditions. To be an information source.

Activities   Sponsoring the Jenny Lind scholarship recipient in Chicago; the Swedish festival at the Botanical Garden; St. Lucia celebration-Chicago; fundraisers for the Swedish America Museum Center.

Publication   SVEA BLADET, a newsletter published nine or ten times a year.

◆ SVEA of Texas

PO Box 53628
Houston, TX 77052
Tel. (713)668-5192 (Carina Leavens)

President   Carina Leavens

Founded   1980

Members   105

Purpose   The purpose of the Club is to keep in close contact with Sweden of today and with the Swedish women in Texas; to stimulate and maintain the Swedish language and cultural traditions, to advertise and support cultural events; to function as a source of information and advice to its members.

Activities   Monthly meetings are held with programs such as speakers, interest groups for music, arts and crafts, cooking, and luncheons; sponsorship of the St. Lucia celebration, an Advent church service, and a Julotta church service.

Publication   SVEA NYTT, a newsletter published five times per year.

◆ SVEA, Washington DC

PO Box 39005
Washington, DC 20016
Tel. (301)493-8835 (Gunilla Stone)

President   Gunilla Stone

Founded   1981

Members   267

Purpose   The purpose of the organization is to keep close contact with Sweden and with Swedes in the Washington area, to encourage the use of the Swedish language and to preserve the Swedish culture and traditions as well as to provide information about the current political and cultural situation in Sweden. The only requirement for membership is fluency in the Swedish language.

Activities   The organization has a lending library and reading room with Swedish periodicals and newspapers. Lectures are given by visiting Swedish people in the arts, screenings of Swedish movies when possible, and art exhibits.

Publication   SVEA-JOURNALEN, a quarterly newsletter.

◆ Sveaborg

c/o Osten Magneheim
6101 Loch Raven Boulevard, #616
Baltimore, MD 21239
Tel. (301)532-6630

President   Margot Beall

Founded   1950

Members   119

Purpose   The purpose of the organization is to provide a means for persons of Swedish descent, persons who are Swedish by marriage, and/or people interested in Sweden to meet, socialize, and preserve some Swedish traditions.

Activities   Midsummer fest; St. Lucia celebration; smörgåsbord; lectures; films; and other social events.

Svensk Hyllningsfest, Inc.

c/o Dorene Anderson
Lindsborg Chamber of Commerce
PO Box 323
Lindsborg, KS 67456
Tel. (913)227-3706

Co-chairs   Bill Taylor, Jr. and Nancy B. Peterson

Founded   1941

Purpose   The purpose of the organization is to pay tribute to the Swedish pioneers who settled in the Smoky Valley; to emphasize the Swedish influence which has dominated the community and made possible its rich heritage; to support activities in the community in education, heritage, music, arts and crafts, Swedish festivals, and recreation.

Activities   Activities of the group include study and research of the Swedish immigration, hosting visiting groups and arranging public events to promote celebrations. Every two years, in the fall, a Swedish festival is held in conjunction with Bethany College's homecoming. This event is usually held in the October of the odd year (1991, 1993, etc.)

Publications A Festival brochure is supplemented by an off-year informational brochure and a souvenir booklet (40+ pages) which focuses on the heritage and ethnic traditions within the Smoky Valley.

Svenska Bokklubben

50 Pine Street
Wellesley, MA 02181
Tel. (617)235-6463 (Sylvia Bullock)

Coordinator Sylvia Bullock

Founded   1974

Members   80 members in 7 groups

Purpose   To share, purchase, read, and discuss current Swedish literature.

Svenska Gillet

c/o Gunnar Seaberg
2234 W. Greenleaf Avenue
Chicago, IL 60645
Tel. (312)973-4112

President   Steve Bergstrom

Founded   1951

Members   80

Purpose   The purpose of the organization is a friendship club.

Svenska Klubben

c/o Raili Marcilla
1012 Guadalupe del Prado
Albuquerque, NM 87107
Tel. (505)345-5424

Founded   1984

Members   14

Purpose   To preserve and promote Swedish culture and language.

Activities Monthly meetings; celebration of Swedish holidays; participation in the Scandinavian Summerfest in Albuquerque.

Svenska Kulturföreningen

c/o Lawrence Wahlstrom
110 Skyline Drive
Eau Claire, WI 54703
Tel. (715)834-1504

President   Lawrence Wahlstrom

Founded   1950

Purpose   To present programs on Sweden, primarily, but also on the other Scandinavian countries. We want people to know more about Swedish culture.

Svenska Societeten (The Swedish Society of New York)

c/o S. William Olson
321 Garden City Road
Franklin Square, NY 11010
Tel. (516)352-0807

President   S. William Olson

Founded   1836

Members   106

Purpose   The Swedish Society of New York is the oldest Swedish-American organization in the United States. The group's ambition is to keep the Society alive for as many years as possible.

Activities   The Society's activities include social events, films, and concerts. In 1986, to celebrate the 150th anniversary of the Society, a two-week trip to Sweden was made by some of its members.

Svenska Sällskapet

c/o American Swedish Institute
2600 Park Avenue
Minneapolis, MN 55407
Tel. (612)871-4907

President   Dennis D. Johnson

Founded   1926

Members   100. Membership is limited to 100 men of Swedish birth or descent.

Purpose   The organization's purpose is to gather together like-minded men for the promotion of things Swedish.

Activities   The Club's social activities include monthly dinners; Midsummer party; Winter party; annual golf tourney; annual fishing trip; and regular meetings from September to May.

Svenska Sällskapets Sällskap

c/o Lilly Gustafson
Rt. 2, Box 139A
Buffalo, MN 55313
Tel. (612)682-4438

President   Lilly Gustafson

Founded   1932

Members   65. The club's membership consists of wives of the group's parent organization, Svenska Sällskapet.

Purpose   The Sällskap is an auxiliary to Svenska Sällskapet, to promote Swedish culture; basically a social organization.

Activities   They have two meetings per year, an annual meeting in May, a field trip, and a Christmas luncheon at the American Swedish Institute.

◆ Svenska Vänner

c/o Winifred Townsend
3 Riverview Lane
Jamestown, ND 58401
Tel. (701)252-6482

Advisory Board   Ted Voigt, William Soper, Helen Hample, Winifred Townsend

Founded   1985

Members   95

Purpose   To bring together persons with Swedish roots who are scattered around East Central North Dakota in order for them to renew an appreciation of their Swedish heritage; to share Swedish traditions, to learn about contributions made by Swedish immigrants to this country, and to learn more about past and present Sweden.

Activities   Tretondag Jul celebration; annual Midsummer party; and offering of Swedish language classes for beginners.

Publication   SVENSKA VÄNNER, a newsletter.

◆ Svenska Vännerna, Inc.

c/o Kathy Lee
Box 397
Sherburn, MN 56171
Tel. (507)764-7181

Founded   1979

Members   123

Purpose   To promote all aspects of Swedish and Swedish-American heritage and culture.

Activities   A festival of St. Lucia; a Midsummer celebration; other social events.

Svenskarnas Dag

c/o Audrey Landquist
4505 Abbott Avenue N.
Minneapolis, MN 55422
Tel. (612)537-6330

President   Harlan Berntson

Founded   1933

Members   Approximately 125 delegates from 35 other Swedish organizations.

Purpose   The organization arranges and promotes a day-long celebration at Minnehaha Park in Minneapolis, MN on the Sunday closest to Midsummer for the purpose of bringing Swedes together. Visiting Swedish groups and dignitaries are part of the celebration.

Activities   The group's activities center on Svenskarnas Dag and a St. Lucia celebration, plus other programs during the year.

Affiliate

Svenskarnas Dag All Girl Choir
c/o Audrey Landquist, Manager and Accompanist
4505 Abbott Avenue N.
Minneapolis, MN 55422

The Choir, founded in 1967, is comprised of 25 young women (ages 10-22) who perform at various functions for the purpose of perpetuating Swedish music and songs. The Choir has given concert tours in many states and five times in Sweden. Diane Noble is the Director.

◆ SWEA International, Inc. (Swedish Women's Educational Association)

PO Box 2585
La Jolla, CA 92037
Tel. (619)459-8435 or 587-0807
Fax (619)597-4111

President   Kerstin Mayberry

Founded   1979

Members   3,700

Purpose   SWEA International is a non-profit organization, a global network of Swedish women. The purpose of the group is to support and maintain Swedish culture and traditions. SWEA consists of 30 chapters in the United States, Canada, Europe, Asia, and South America. SWEA International is the umbrella organization serving all chapters.

Activities   Christmas bazaars; dinners with guest speakers, and other fund raising events. SWEA International also gives scholarships to graduate students of the Swedish language and literature.

Chapters (United States and Canada)

Arizona
Carin Coleridge, President
11644 N. 52nd Street
Scottsdale, AZ 85254
(602)996-6932

Boston
Ilona E. Ferraro, President
42 Kirkland Circle
Wellesley Hills, MA 02181
(617)235-6755

Buffalo (subchapter to New York)
Louise Enhörning, President
21 Oakland Place
Buffalo, NY 14222
(716)822-3626

Denver
Karin Strook, President
12363 West Saratoga Avenue
Morrison, CO 80465
(303)979-4254

Hawaii
Helena Cence, President
1071 Noio Street
Honolulu, HI 96816
(808)737-0030

Los Angeles
Marianne Färm-Reinholds, President
4444 Los Feliz Blvd., #108
Los Angeles, CA 90027
(213)663-0753

Michigan
Tottie Samuelson, President
6055 Braemoor Trail
Birmingham, MI 48010
(313)626-7822

New Jersey
Margareta Ugander, President
59 Heritage Court
Woodcliff Lake, NJ 07675
(201)391-2303

New York
Ulla Fredsvik Konvalin, President
147 E. 82nd Street, #2B
New York, NY 10028
(212)517-6029

Orange County
Marianne Friedman, President
12 Rustling Wind
Irvine, CA 92715
(714)854-2855

San Diego
Gunnel Schoenherr, President
11423 Lucera Place
San Diego, CA 92127
(619)485-8706

San Francisco
Siv Winberg-Losey, President
PO Box 586
Nicasio, CA 94946
(415)662-2300

Santa Barbara (subchapter to Los Angeles)
Elise Koelsch, President
729 N. Voluntario Street
Santa Barbara, CA 93103
(805)965-4097

Seattle
Ingrid Ahlman, President
22223 N.E. 62nd Place
Redmond, WA 98053
(206)868-6447

Toronto
Inga Ingram, President
3434 Eglinton Avenue E., #1702
Scarborough, ON L3P 3B5 Canada
(416)264-3875

Vancouver
Gisela Edstrand, President
VM PO Box 4591
Vancouver, BC V6B 4A1 Canada
(604)926-6871

Swedish American Athletic Association, Inc.

c/o Woodrow W. Eisenhart
243 East 113th Street
Chicago, IL 60628
Tel. (312)785-7589

President   Roy A. Swanson
Founded   1914
Members   150 men only

Purpose   The object and purpose of the Association is to unite men of Swedish birth or descent, of sound health and good character; to aid, promote, and advance Swedish gymnastics and all indoor and outdoor athletic sports and in general work for the social, moral, and intellectual welfare and advancement of the Association and its members.

Activities   The Association now sponsors two bowling teams and two golf clubs. They also celebrate Swedish holidays and enjoy various social activities.

Swedish American Central Association of Southern California

Dr. Jacqueline E. Ahlen, Secretary
PO Box 40579
Pasadena, CA 91114
Tel. (818)794-0729

President   Gost I. Ahlen

Founded   1920

Members   45 delegates representing 15 Swedish-American organizations.

Purpose   To preserve the Swedish culture, customs, and heritage. To act as an umbrella organization for other Swedish organizations.

Activities   Sponsors and arranges an annual Midsummer festival; provides hospitality for visiting Swedish-American cultural activities and group tours.

Swedish-American Chamber of Commerce of the United States, Inc. (SACC US)

In 1991 chambers of commerce are in operation in the following cities in the United States: Atlanta, Boston, Chicago, Denver, Detroit, Fort Lauderdale, Houston, Los Angeles, New York, San Diego, San Francisco, Seattle, Tampa Bay, and Washington DC. All these chambers belong to SACC US. The New York Chamber serves as a secretariat for the national organization. Olle Wijkstrom, is the executive secretary of SACC US.

◆ Swedish-American Chamber of Commerce, Inc. (Houston Chapter)

PO Box 243
Bellaire, TX 77402
Tel. (713)660-8700
Fax (713)667-7300

President   James E. Leavens

Founded   1983

Members   74

Purpose   To enhance trade and commerce between the United
States and Sweden.

Activities   Business luncheons with different guest speakers.

Publication   A joint newsletter with New York City.

◆ Swedish-American Chamber of Commerce, Inc. (New York Chapter)

599 Lexington Avenue
New York, NY 10022
Tel. (212)838-5530

President   Olle Wijkstrom

Founded   1906

Members   800

Purpose   The Swedish-American Chamber of Commerce is an
independent, private, and nonprofit organization, established to
develop mutually prosperous and friendly economic, social, and
commercial relations between business and industrial interests in
the United States and Sweden.

Activities   Forums, seminars, conferences, and other special events
to provide the members with opportunities to exchange ideas and
opinions on major issues. The Chamber also provides research and
information services and maintains a specialized library. It also
provides counseling or direct assistance to visitors, and sponsors
social activities.

Publications An ANNUAL REPORT & MEMBERSHIP DIRECTORY
which includes trade statistics, useful addresses in Sweden, etc; a

newsletter, SWEDISH HOLIDAYS AND HOLIDAYS IN THE U.S.A.;
the book, SWEDISH RELATED COMPANIES IN THE U.S.A.; the
directory, YELLOW PAGES, listing companies providing special
services; and several booklets on subjects of interest to the Swedish-
American business community.

◆ Swedish-American Chamber of Commerce of the Western United States, Inc.

230 California Street, Suite 602
San Francisco, CA 94111-4319
Tel. (415)781-4188

Chairman   Siri M. Eliason

Founded   1947

Members   200

Purpose   To promote healthy two-way trade between Sweden and
the Western United States.

Activities Regular luncheon meetings; annual Christmas luncheon;
golf tournament; crayfish party.

Publication A quarterly newsletter.

◆ The Swedish American Council of Boston

c/o Ruth E. Setterberg
770 Boylston Street
Boston, MA 02199

President   Wendell N. Gustafson

Founded   1943

Members   125-150

Purpose   The Swedish American Council of Boston aims to preserve and share the rich cultural life and traditions of Sweden; to
develop understanding of the role of Sweden in world history, past
and present; to strengthen relations between the United States and
Sweden; and to serve as a resource center of information. It aims to
foster educational and cultural exchange between the two countries; and to provide opportunities for the community to participate
in programs of excellence and holiday celebrations. Since its

founding the Council has been affiliated with the Consulate of Sweden in Boston.

Activities   The Council presents lectures by distinguished Swedish and Swedish-American leaders on subjects of historical interest. It offers concerts, films, and exhibits. At receptions and dinners it recognizes Swedish and Swedish-American leaders of distinction who have contributed notably to the cultural life of the United States, Sweden, and other nations. It collects and forwards information requested by scholars engaged in Swedish-American studies. It develops funds for an annual scholarship to be awarded to a student from Sweden studying at Mount Ida College. At Christmas all Swedish students attending universities and colleges in the Greater Boston area are guests of the Council at a St. Lucia fest and smörgåsbord. The Council enriches activities by including other Swedish-American organizations, by incorporating traditional aspects, and by sharing information and announcements sent by Swedish Council of America and the Swedish Information Service.

◆ Swedish-American Cultural Union

c/o Bo B. Jonsson, Board Chairman
3525 Grace Street N.W., Suite 109
Washington, DC 20007

President   Dr. Harlan Strauss

Founded   1975-76

Members   250

Purpose   This is basically a luncheon group with emphasis on speakers and topics in economics, politics, culture, and business fields which emphasize current Swedish-American relations and views.

Activities   Lectures, concerts, and holiday celebrations.

Publication   A newsletter.

◆ Swedish American Historical Association of California

c/o California Lutheran University
60 W. Olsen Road
Thousand Oaks, CA 91360
Tel. (805)495-7274 (Aina Abrahamson)

President   Barbro Hoeglund

Founded   1977

Members   500

Purpose   The Swedish community of California has a rich background of historical significance that is unique. So that this heritage will not in time be diffused or distorted, the Swedish American Historical Association of California desires that these historical records and events be preserved for posterity as a source of inspiration and enrichment.

Activities   Taping interviews with Swedish pioneers in California; collecting memorabilia of Swedish origin; gathering funds to develop a Heritage Center; and gathering information about sites and people significant in the history of Swedes in California.

Publication   ALMANAC, a newsletter.

◆ Swedish-American Historical Society

5125 N. Spaulding Avenue
Chicago, IL 60625
Tel. (312)583-5722

President   Philip J. Anderson

Founded   1948

Members   1300

Purpose   The Society's purpose is to record the achievements of the Swedish pioneers and to stimulate and promote interest in Swedish and Swedish-American contributions to the development and life of the United States of America; to preserve and collect documents and general data of historical interest; to encourage and promote Swedish-American historical research and literary work and publish pamphlets, monographs, magazines, books, and other works; to maintain and further develop cultural exchange between America and Sweden; and to promote the general interest among Americans of pioneer heritage.

Activities   The Society's activities include conferences on immigration history, social events, the sale of books related to the organization's purpose, domestic tours and Scandinavian tours, and public events such as films, lectures, and exhibits. The Society also operates the Swedish-American Archives of Greater Chicago, which involves the collection and microfilming of published and unpublished materials relating to Swedish-America.

Publications THE SWEDISH-AMERICAN HISTORICAL QUARTERLY; books.

Affiliate

> **Swedish Committee, Swedish-American**
> **Historical Society (Sweden)**
> Dr. Harald Runblom
> Center for Multi-Ethnic Studies
> Sankt Johannesgatan 21
> S-752 35 Uppsala
> SWEDEN
> Tel. 011 46 18 13 55 83

> The Committee carries out the purpose of the Swedish-American Historical Society among its members in Sweden, and supports the publication of the SWEDISH-AMERICAN HISTORICAL QUARTERLY published by the Society.

Swedish-American Historical Society of Wisconsin

c/o Janice Touve, Secretary
7236 S. 35th Street
Franklin, WI 53132
Tel. (414)421-0666

President   Victor Hedman

Founded   1974

Members   83

Purpose   The primary objective of the Swedish-American Historical Society of Wisconsin is to gather and preserve the history of Swedish immigrants to Wisconsin.

Activities   Establishment of a historical marker in memory and honor of the first Swedish family who settled in Wisconsin, the Friman family which settled in Genoa City near the Wisconsin/Illinois state line. The marker was dedicated June 4, 1988.

On September 21, 1991, the Society dedicated a historical marker at Nashotah House Episcopal Seminary to honor the memory of Gustaf Unonius, who immigrated to Wisconsin in 1841. Unonius was the first graduate of Nashotah House, which was the first Episcopal Seminary established in Wisconsin.

Programs, at quarterly membership meetings, about specific Swedish-American persons who have been influential in Wisconsin industry, civic leadership, and Wisconsin and United States government; special programs pertaining to Swedish culture and traditions; in addition the Society organizes a Midsummer fest at Old World, Wisconsin.

Publication   A quarterly newsletter for the members.

Associate

> **Linde Lodge #492 - Vasa Order of America**
> Les Touve, Chairman
> 7236 S. 35th Street
> Franklin, WI 53132
> (414)421-0666

◆ The Swedish American Museum Center of Chicago (SAMAC)

5211 N. Clark Street
Chicago, IL 60640
Tel. (312)728-8111
Fax (312)728-8870

President   Tomas Bergman

Executive Director   Kerstin B. Lane

Founded   1976

Members   1,300

Purpose   The purpose of SAMAC is to collect, restore, and display artifacts relating to the Swedish immigration to Chicago; to maintain a library consistent with the purpose of the Center; to preserve and celebrate the Swedish heritage through exhibits, lectures, and observation of special holidays; to act as a source of information on

Sweden; and to become a center for Swedish activities in the Chicago area.

Activities   Lectures; concerts; movies; St. Lucia celebration; Mid-summer celebration. Also workshops in Swedish crafts, language, and genealogy are held. In addition to the permanent exhibit on Swedish Immigration to Chicago, the Museum Center hosts temporary exhibits of Swedish art and crafts, and famous Swedish personalities.

Publication   SAMAC NEWS, a newsletter.

Swedish Art Institute

Kirstin D. Lipka
8383 East Evans Road
Scottsdale, AZ 85260-3614
Tel. (602)998-2000
Fax (602)998-8022

**Executive
Director**   Robert G. Johnson

Founded   1991

Purpose   The Swedish Art Institute will display and promote Swedish visual art, both contemporary and historical in nature. Endorsing Swedish art is SAI's principal intention, with the secondary purpose of promoting the country of Sweden.

Publications A quarterly newsletter; annual catalog.

◆ The Swedish Club

1612 Waugh Drive
Houston, TX 77006
Tel. (713)522-5552

President   Dr. Birger Jansson

Founded   1986

Members   242

Purpose   The purpose of the Club is to preserve Swedish traditions and culture.

Activities   Educational and social.

Publication   THE SWEDISH CLUB NEWS, a quarterly newsletter.

◆ Swedish Club, Inc.

1920 Dexter Avenue N.
Seattle, WA 98109
Tel. (206)283-1090 or 283-1077

President   Bertil O. Lundh

**Contact
person**   Ingrid Karlsson, Director

Founded   1892

Members   The membership is comprised of people who are either
of Scandinavian extraction or married to a Scandinavian.

Purpose   The Club's purpose is to promote a better understanding
between the United States and Scandinavia, and to perpetuate
Scandinavian culture and traditions; to maintain its own building
with facilities for members' enjoyment and convenience; to give
moral as well as financial support to worthy projects, when so
deemed proper.

Activities   Language and craft classes; singing; folk dancing; lectures; concerts; films; exhibits; and social events (salmon bakes,
crayfish parties, Midsummerfest, St. Lucia, etc.)

Publication   SWEDISH CLUB NEWS, a newsletter.

◆ The Swedish Club of Denver

c/o Per Karlqvist
5118 S. Broadway
Englewood, CO 80110
Tel. (303)761-3285

President   Norman Lundin

Founded   1958

Members   326

Purpose   The purpose of the Club is to promote and preserve
Swedish customs and heritage.

Activities   Colorado Folk Arts; picnics; monthly dinners; St. Lucia
celebration; Midsummer celebration.

Publication   TRE KRONOR (Three Crowns), a newsletter.

◆ Swedish Club of Los Angeles

c/o Carl G. Lindquist
20827 Exhibit Place
Woodland Hills, CA 90046

President   Carl G. Lindquist

Founded   1922

Members   140

Purpose   To foster the customs and ties of the many Swedes and Swedish descendants in the Los Angeles area; to assist in the preservation of the Swedish heritage through events; and with scholarship funds provide for students and institutions who are involved in these activites.

Activities   Throughout the year the Swedish Club holds meetings and events which stress Swedish customs and traditions, culminating with the annual Christmas ball and scholarship awards in December.

◆ Swedish Club of Metropolitan Detroit

22398 Ruth Street
Farmington Hills, MI 48336
Tel. (313)478-2563

President   Thomas Wilkinson

Founded   1953

Members   375

Purpose   To preserve, foster, and perpetuate the traditions, customs, and culture of Scandinavia in general and the Swedish heritage in particular; to maintain a spirit of kinship among the Swedish and Scandinavian-American community in the metropolitan Detroit area; to serve cultural, social, educational, charitable, and civic purposes. The Swedish club also sponsors, encourages, and supports the Arpi Male Chorus and the Scandia Women's chorus, thereby furthering the interest in and preserving the traditions of Swedish singing.

Activities   Swedish language, cooking, and baking classes; singing concerts; Midsummer festival; women's organization functions; Retirees' club; monthly brunches; Swedish pancake breakfasts; St. Lucia-lutfisk dinner, children's Christmas party; Dopp-i-grytan dinner; Ägg-sexa; venison dinner; Mother's Day luncheon; Steak and corn roast; plus many other events during the year.

Publication   A bimonthly newsletter.

◆ Swedish Club of San Francisco and Bay Area

PO Box 494
San Carlos, CA 94070
Tel. (415)969-1515

President   Ernst A. Jensen

Founded   1913

Members   290. Membership is restricted to those of Swedish birth or Swedish descent.

Purpose   The Club's purpose is to keep up Swedish traditions and culture.

Activities   Activities include educational programs, social functions, and holiday celebrations.

Publication   NYHETS BULLETIN, a newsletter.

◆ Swedish Club of Sarasota

c/o Ragnar Swanson
PO Box 21722
Sarasota, FL 34242
Tel. (813)349-3929

President   Anita Boakes

Founded   1988

Members   176

Purpose   The Swedish Club of Sarasota was established for the purpose of providing integration and preservation of Swedish culture in the community.

Activities   A pea soup dinner; a Walpurgis night; a Midsummer festival; a fall crayfish dinner; a St. Lucia festival.

Swedish Club Women's Organization

22398 Ruth Street
Farmington Hills, MI 48336
Tel. (313)478-2563

President   Barbara Showalter

Founded   1984

Members   20

Purpose   To support the activities of the Swedish Club of Metropolitan Detroit and to preserve our Swedish heritage.

Activities   The Organization sponsors an annual bazaar, a Lutfisk dinner, a St. Lucia program, and a Dopp-i-gryttan. They assist with the Midsummer celebration.

◆ The Swedish Colonial Society

1300 Locust Street
Philadelphia, PA 19107
Tel. (215)732-6200

Governor   Wallace F. Richter

Founded   1908

Members   320

Purpose   The purpose of the Society is to collect, preserve, and publish records, documents and other material, printed or in manuscript, and to commemorate events relating to the history of the Swedes in America, and to acquire, receive, and own real estate for the purpose of its incorporation, and to have, hold, and own real estate and personal property for the maintenance of parks, monuments, memorials and tablets, locating, fixing and determining historical sites, and to commemorate historical events and accomplishments.

Activities   Excursions to places of special historical interest, observation of important historical events such as the issuance of a commemorative stamp of the Treaty of Friendship and Commerce between the United States and Sweden in 1983.

Publications Numerous books, booklets, and articles in newspapers. Recently this includes THE NAVAL CAMPAIGN OF COUNT DE GRASSE AMERICAN REVOLUTION 1781-1783 by Karl Gustaf Törnquist, translated from the Swedish by Amandus Johnson, published 1983. Newsletter, two issues per year.

◆ Swedish Conversation Club

c/o Joan Tucker
1600 Prairie du Chien Road
Iowa City, IA 52245
Tel. (319)354-1631
or
c/o Kathleen Armens
31 Brookfield Drive
Iowa City, IA 52240
Tel. (319)338-2675

Founded   1978

Members   33

Purpose   The purpose of the club is to join together people who are interested in Sweden, Swedish culture, and language.

Activities   Celebrations of St. Lucia, Valborgsmässafton, and Midsummer as well as films and language classes.

Publication   A newsletter.

Swedish Council Around North Dakota

c/o Rev. Les Wassberg
2126 S. 11th Street
Fargo, ND 58103
Tel. (701)280-0956

Convener   Reverend Les Wassberg

Founded   1989

Members   Five member groups

Purpose   To organize an annual gathering; to share information, programs, and occasional group activities in North Dakota.

Activities   Spring convocation luncheon; sponsoring students to Swedish Language Village.

Member Groups

Lake Regions Swedish Heritage Society - Devils Lake, ND

Svenska Vänner - Jamestown/Kulm, ND

Swedish Cultural Heritage Society of the Red River Valley - Fargo, ND/Moorhead, MN

Three Crowns American Swedish Association - Bismarck, ND

A new group in Minot, ND

◆ Swedish Council of Saint Louis

c/o Elton Tonsing
400 Tamarack Drive
Ballwin, MO 63011
Tel. (314)394-3802

President   Philip Graham

Founded   1976

Members   100 families

Purpose   The Council's purpose is to promote knowledge and
understanding of the Swedish heritage in American life and to
strengthen the cultural ties between the United States and Sweden.
The objectives are to promote social, educational, and cultural
activities which will enhance the Swedish-American heritage in St.
Louis.

Activities   St. Lucia festival; Valborgsmässafton; Potatiskorv supper; Midsummer celebration; Julotta; picnic; and other social events.

Publication   GULT OCH BLÅTT, a newsletter.

Swedish Council of Winston-Salem

c/o Earl Fredrik Lindberg
1020 Turtle Rock Lane
Winston-Salem, NC 27104
Tel. (919)768-9027

Founded   1984

Activities   An annual St. Lucia and Christmas smörgåsbord; crayfish party.

The Swedish Cultural Association of Manitoba, Inc.

Göran Hedenstierna
764 Erin Street
Winnipeg, Manitoba, R3G 2W4
CANADA
Tel. (204)774-8047

President   Göran (George) Hedenstierna

Founded   1983

Members   51

Purpose   To promote the preservation of the Swedish culture and language in Manitoba; to promote interaction in the Winnipeg area between people of Swedish origin and others that are interested to be associated with what is Sweden; to act as liaison with similar Swedish association throughout Canada and the United States; to assist as much as possible in the undertaking of local events sponsored by Swedish individuals or groups, authorities, or corporations, if such events are compatible with the aims and objectives of the Association.

Activities   Display of an information booth in the Scandinavian Centre's pavilion during Winnipeg's Folklorama events; Scandinavian Midsummer fest at the Swedish Vasalund in Winnipeg; hosting a Swedish Pee Wee Ice Hockey team from Trelleborg at the Swedish Easter Sunday brunch at the Scandinavian Centre; hosting the Swedish Women's and Men's 1991 Curling Champions at the Scandinavian Centre; a St. Lucia pageant in December.

Publications SWEDES AND SWEDE LIKES; one page (Svenska Sidan) in the Viking Times, published five times a year.

◆ Swedish Cultural Committee, Inc.

c/o Donald H. Erickson
10330 Regency Parkway Drive
Omaha, NE 68114

President   Donald H. Erickson

Founded   November 12, 1989

Members   20

Purpose   To focus attention on Swedish contributions to the intellectual, cultural, and commercial life in the state of Nebraska and in the United States in general, and to highlight aspects of historical and modern Sweden as well. The goal is not only to heighten awareness of Sweden and Swedish influence in the United States, but also to enhance trade, travel, and intellectual ties between the two countries.

Activities   Sponsoring a continuing education program in cooperation with the University of Nebraska at Omaha in language, arts, history, and genealogy; sponsoring visits of Swedish government officials and diplomats to Nebraska.

Publication   SWEDES IN OMAHA, a compilation of historical and biographical data of Swedish families, institutions, and businesses in Omaha.

◆ The Swedish Cultural Heritage Society of the Red River Valley

PO Box 1132
Fargo, ND 58107
Tel. (701)232-1390 (Dallas Young)

President   Dallas Young

Founded   1976

Members   300

Purpose   The purpose of the Society is to enrich the members' lives with the charm and beauty of Swedish culture; to increase awareness and understanding of modern Sweden in the community; to contribute tangibly to the Swedish cultural presence in the area served by the Society.

Activities   Feature films; art exhibits; concerts; lectures on Swedish and Swedish-American subjects; Swedish classes; excursions to places of Swedish interest; and traditional festivals such as St. Lucia, Midsummer, and Valborg.

Publication   VÅR DAL, a newsletter published six times per year.

◆ Swedish Cultural Society in America

c/o Sven Sjostedt
PO Box 8042
St. Paul, MN 55108
Tel. (612)645-8578

President   Sven Sjostedt

Members   1,000

Purpose   The Society's purpose is to support and promote efforts
to sustain the Swedish language and culture among the Swedish
people and their descendants in America, specifically in unity with
the Swedish-American press, Swedish organizations, churches, fraternal groups, and singing societies. An important part of the
activity of the Society is to spread knowledge of Sweden, Swedish
life, and Swedish literature and culture among the American people.

Activities   Most of the local organizations have public meetings
every month. At that time high quality programs are presented with
lectures, songs, and musical entertainment. Chartered trips are
taken to familiarize the members with the history of Swedish
immigration to America and the contributions of Swedish pioneers
to America. The Society also encourages its members in gathering
and preserving historical Swedish documents, photos, and other
items of interest to future generations.

Publication   KULTURARVET-SWEDISH HERITAGE, a newsletter.

Affiliate

◆   **Rikföreningen Sverigekontakt (The National Association for
Contact with Sweden)**
c/o Dr. Lennart Limberg
Box 53066
S-400 14 Göteborg
SWEDEN

Chapters

Chicago
Per-Hugo Kristensson, President
1123 S. Courtland Avenue
Park Ridge, IL 60068

Northern California
Virginia Campbell, President
4274 Nando Court
Castro Valley, CA 94546

◆ **Cleveland**
Bo Carlsson, President
2708 Rochester Road
Shaker Heights, OH 44122

Duluth
Clifford Hedman, President
4410 Gilliat Street
Duluth, MN 55804

Eau Claire
Lawrence F. Wahlstrom, President
110 Skyline Drive
Eau Claire, WI 54701

Minneapolis-St. Paul
Leslie Flink, President
1150 Lois Court
Shoreview, MN 55126

New York
Viola Spongberg-Holmberg, President
PO Box 177
Thornwood, NY 10594

◆ **Rockford**
William Johnson
411 Welty Avenue
Rockford, IL 61107

Seattle
Filippa Engqvist, President
557 Lake Washington Road E.
Seattle, WA 98112

Vancouver
Britta Norman
1320 East Hastings Street
Vancouver, BC V5L 1S3 Canada

◆ Swedish Cultural Society of Cleveland

c/o Bo Carlsson
2708 Rochester Road
Shaker Heights, OH 44122
Tel. (216)464-1794

President   Bo Carlsson

Founded   October 28, 1927

Members   43

Purpose   To fulfill the need for people of Swedish national origin to get together on the common ground of their love of Scandinavian traditions, and to celebrate activities and holidays.

Activities   St. Lucia fest; Tjugondag Knut party; wine tasting party; trivia questions and slides from Sweden; singing of traditional Swedish songs; Midsummer celebration; presentations of Swedish companies in Cleveland; travel reports; presentations by invited speakers.

Swedish Cultural Society of Northern California

c/o Susan Nelson, Secretary
144 Alta Road
Oakland, CA 94618
Tel. (415)653-8897

President   Inez A. Rhodin

Founded   1950

Members   46

Purpose   To provide education and culture for its members.

Activities   A 40th anniversary banquet; a St. Lucia festival; a Twelfth Night dinner; the showing of the movie *Babette's Feast*; emphasis - Norrland.

◆ Swedish Cultural Society of Rockford

c/o Ann Sandquist
2929 Sunnyside Drive
Rockford, IL 61111-6021

President   William Johnson

Founded   December 15, 1950

Members   125

Purpose   To create a bond between Swedes and Swedish descendants residing in the area. To rekindle, sustain, and strengthen interest in and love of Swedish culture in its various forms. To preserve the Swedish language to the greatest possible extent.

Activities   Participation in the celebration of 350 years, both in Rockford and Chicago; Gustaf Adolph fest in Chicago in the fall; joint Christmas fest in Chicago in December and in Rockford in January. Meetings are held the second Sunday of every month September through May at the Tabor Lutheran Church in Rockford.

Publication   ARVET, (published in Minneapolis).

◆ Swedish Culture Society

c/o Steve Clayton
229 15th Avenue S.W.
Largo, FL 34640-7501
Tel. (813)581-8445

President   Christina Wirebjer

Founded   1981

Members   118

Purpose   To preserve and promote Swedish culture, customs, and tradition. To inform the public and to provide educational services through local schools.

Activities   Involvement in the International Folk Fair, Great Explorations, local parades and celebrations; ongoing support of Swedish exchange students.

Publication   A monthly newsletter.

The Swedish Festival

Judy Buzek, Chamber of Commerce Secretary
PO Box 353SCA
Stromsburg, NE 68666
Tel. (402)764-2111

President   Marvin Wadell, Chamber of Commerce

Founded   1952, first festival

Purpose   The Swedish Festival was begun to celebrate Midsummer Day. Today it has grown to a three-day event held annually on the third weekend in June. The Festival attracts 5,000 to 10,000 people annually. At the 1966 Swedish Festival, Nebraskan Governor, Frank Morrison, proclaimed Stromsburg as "The Swede Capital of Nebraska".

Activities   Festival events include a Swedish craft shop, free entertainment, parades, Art in the Park where exhibitors show and sell
arts and crafts in the city square, and an authentic Swedish
smörgåsbord.

Swedish Folk Dance Club of Los Angeles

Per-Olof Karlsson
347 N. Myrtle Avenue
Monrovia, CA 91016
Tel. (818)359-1549

President   Per-Olof (Perry) Karlsson

Founded   1916

Members   20

Purpose   The purpose of the Club is to promote Swedish folk
dancing in order to preserve this very important aspect of Swedish
culture. All the members have authentic Swedish costumes and
perform dances as they have been done in Sweden for hundreds of
years.

Activities   They perform dances for several organizations throughout the year - Swedish and otherwise. They have performed at the
Los Angeles Music Center, in Sweden, Las Vegas, and for various
holiday celebrations in the Los Angeles area.

Swedish Folkdancers of New York

c/o Yvonne Holland
222 W. 83rd Street, Box 85
New York, NY 10024
Tel. (212)877-5082

President   Richard Haggblad

Founded   1906

Members   50

Purpose   The organization's purpose is to spread the knowledge
of and awaken the interest in traditional Swedish culture, particularly its folk dances, folk games, and holiday celebrations.

Activities   Folk dancing; dance games; weekly dance instruction
and rehearsals. They also perform at local festivals throughout the
Eastern Seaboard.

Swedish Genealogy Group

c/o Minnesota Genealogical Society
PO Box 16069
St. Paul, MN 55116-0069
Tel. (612)222-6929 (Minnesota Genealogical Society)

President   Fran Hillier

Founded   1983

Members   100

Purpose   The Swedish Genealogy Group is a subgroup of the Scandinavian-American Genealogical Society. The purposes of the group are to help solve individual problems with all the members contributing solutions; to research the more common trouble areas; to hold meetings for the instruction and encouragement of the members; to provide informative talks on some facet of genealogy; to publish materials. The group acts as a liaison between Americans looking for their Swedish roots, and Swedes looking for their American relatives.

Activities   Recent activities include the indexing of marriage and death records of Swedish newspapers published in Minneapolis and St. Paul during 1800s and early 1900s.

Publications SWEDISH GENEALOGICAL RESOURCES and SWEDISH GENEALOGICAL DICTIONARY

◆ Swedish Heritage Center

Elsie Sebberson, Curator
301 N. Charde Avenue
Oakland, NE 68045
Tel. (402)685-5041

President   Rev. H. Alan Eagle

Founded   March 1, 1989

Members   350

Purpose   To preserve, display, and teach Oakland's historic past, especially its reflection of Swedish culture; to coordinate and promote tourism and cultural events in the Oakland area, building on its Swedish identity; to expedite the planning and development of programs that will enable Oakland to be recognized as a Swedish heritage center.

Activities   Operation of a museum and gift shop; taking an active part in the community's Swedish festival; sponsorship of lectures on Swedish immigration and settlement in Nebraska; sponsorship of workshops on tracing Swedish genealogy.

Publications A periodic newsletter and publicity brochures.

◆ Swedish Heritage Society

c/o Jane Wickham
PO Box 8
Swedesburg, IA 52652
Tel. (319)254-2193

President   Mrs. Clarence Unkrich

Founded   June 4, 1986

Members   60

Purpose   To gather information about Swedish people who immigrated to Swedesburg and surrounding areas, and to keep a written record of this: to observe Swedish holidays, occasions, and customs; to maintain the Swedish Heritage Museum in Swedesburg.

Activities   St. Lucia fest; bus trips to Bishop Hill, Minneapolis, Rockford, and Decorah; Swedish language lessons; Midsummer fest celebration; providing a smörgåsbord for bus tour groups who visit Swedesburg.

◆ Swedish Heritage Society of Northern Colorado

c/o Elmer Fristrom, Treasurer
1631 10th Avenue
Greeley, CO 80631
Tel. (303)352-7242

President   Violet Carlson

Founded   1977

Members   200

Purpose   The purpose of the Society is to preserve and promote Swedish culture, customs, and specific events.

Activities   Monthly meetings; four smörgåsbord dinners a year; a Christmas Julotta service; observance of Midsummer Day. The Society has also constructed and furnished a Swedish American stuga in Centennial Village in Greeley, Colorado.

◆ Swedish Heritage Society of Utah, Inc.

c/o Curt Dahlén
656 N East Capitol Street
Salt Lake City, UT 84103
Tel. (801)359-4644

President   Curt Dahlén

Founded   May 20, 1982

Members   78

Purpose   To promote the Swedish culture, language, and history in Utah; to introduce persons of Swedish ancestry to traditions of the old country with respect to festivities and foods.

Activities   Monthly meetings; Midsummer; Crayfish party; movie evening; songs and poetry evening; St. Lucia; Walpurgis Eve.

Publications SVENSKA EXPRESSEN, a quarterly newsletter plus a special Christmas issue.

◆ Swedish Historical Society of Rockford

404 S. Third Street
Rockford, IL 61104
Tel. (815)963-5559

President   Per W. Levin

Founded   1939

Members   Approximately 400

Purpose   To collect, preserve, and display items of interest pertaining to the settlement and influence of the Swedish culture in America, and particularly in the Rockford, Illinois, area.

Activities   Celebrations of Midsummer, St. Lucia; an annual picnic; restoration of the Erlander Home Museum.

Swedish Home for the Aged, Inc.

20 Bristol Avenue
Staten Island, NY 10301
Tel. (718)442-1096
Fax (718)442-5376

**President-
Admin.**   Harry V. Hedin

Founded   1909

Purpose   The organization operates a home for elderly Swedish people in metropolitan New York.

Activities   The Home sponsors events, films, lectures, exhibits, and concerts.

Swedish Ladies' Society: Jenny Lind of Oakland

c/o Bertha Bechtle, Secretary
1830 Pearl Street
Alameda, CA 94501
Tel. (415)522-8635

President   Inez A. Rhodin

Founded   1916

Members   93

Purpose   To provide social and sick benefits for their members.

Activities   A 75th anniversary lunch.

The Swedish Ladies Society of San Francisco

Swedish American Hall
2174 Market Street
San Francisco, CA 94114
Tel. (415)664-8642 (Jean Stohl Nelson)

President   Jean Stohl Nelson

Founded   1896

Members   45. Restricted to women of Swedish descent.

Purpose   The Society's purpose is to assist sick members, contribute to funeral expenses of deceased members, and arrange literary and social entertainment.

Activities   The group participates in various Swedish community activities.

The Swedish National Federation

1 Ekman Street
Worcester, MA 01607
Tel. (508)853-6847 (Kristin Sheehan, Secretary)

President   Stig Bjorklund

Founded   1903. Founded as Svensk-Amerikanska Förbundet; in 1911 name changed to Swedish National Federation.

Members   46 delegates from Swedish organizations

Purpose   To preserve and develop the social and cultural heritage that Sweden has bequeathed America; to represent the interests of Swedish descendants.

Activities   A Midsummer Festival; a St. Lucia ball; and scholarship awards.

Member Groups

Kampen Lodge, Independent Order of Good Templars

Quinsigamond Lodge #517, Vasa Order of America

John Ericsson Lodge #25, Vasa Order of America

Nordic Lodge #611, Vasa Order of America

Swedish Folk Dance Club

Fairlawn Foundation

Scandinavian Athletic Club

S.A.C. Ladies' Auxiliary

Swedish Charitable Association

and some contact with the **Salvation Army**

◆ Swedish Northern Lights Society (Nordsken Förening)

c/o Helen McDowell
Box 536
Deer River, MN 56636
Tel. (218)246-8739

President   Helen McDowell

Founded   1979

Members   130

Purpose   To preserve the Swedish heritage including its culture, customs, folk songs, dances, and language; to encourage the young people to develop an interest in their ethnic background.

Activities   A St. Lucia fest in December; a Midsummer picnic in June.

Publication   A bimonthly newsletter.

◆ Swedish Press Society

c/o Anders Neumueller
1294 W. Seventh Avenue
Vancouver, BC V6H 1B6
CANADA
Tel. (609)731-6381

President   Irene Olljum

Founded   November 1928

Members   2,700

Purpose   The organization was formed to secure the continued publication of NYA SVENSKA PRESSEN - SWEDISH PRESS

Activities   Sweden Day (films, lectures, exhibitions, folk dancing etc.).

Publication   NYA SVENSKA PRESSEN - SWEDISH PRESS, a monthly magazine.

Swedish Retirement Association

Gerald C. Parker, Administrator
2320 Pioneer Road
Evanston, IL 60201
Tel. (708)328-8700

President   Irwynn V. Kimball

Founded   1899

Members   250 Association members

Purpose   Swedish Retirement Association combines a gracious, homelike lifestyle with comprehensive lifelong health care services.

Activities   Bible, exercise, and art classes; a walking club; bridge and game time; bingo; shuffleboard; concerts; movies; weekly worship service; shopping trips; day tours; and many other activities.

Publication   TIDINGS, a semiannual newsletter.

Swedish Society Linnea

c/o Paul Anderson
4818 N.E. 37th Avenue
Portland, OR 97211
Tel. (503)281-9895

President   Paul Anderson

Founded   1888

Members   51

Purpose   A social and fraternal organization which provides a meeting place for people mainly of Swedish background.

Activities   A smörgåsbord in February; a Midsummer festival in June; Scanfair in December featuring an array of baked goods and handcrafts.

Swedish Society of Oakland

c/o Robert J. Thiele
265 Lake Drive
Kensington, CA 94708
Tel. (510)524-6150

President   Anders Lundgren

Founded   March 5, 1901

Members   29 (men only)

Activities   For some years meetings have consisted of a short business meeting followed by a social hour.

◆ Swenson Swedish Immigration Research Center

Augustana College
Box 175
Rock Island, IL 61201
Tel. (309)794-7204
Fax (309)794-7443

Swedish-Americans searching for their roots at the Swenson Center in Rock Island, IL.

Director   Dag Blanck

**Archivist &
Managing
Officer**   Kermit Westerberg

Founded   1981

Purpose
1. To collect, arrange, and preserve as completely as possible all books, manuscripts, and letters and related material

pertaining to or growing out of the Swedish immigration to America and its subsequent contribution to American life and culture.

2. To serve as a national archival depository for the records, personal papers, and other documentary material of Swedish-American institutions, organizations, and individuals, regardless of religious, geographical, or organizational origin. Special emphasis will be given to items in danger of being lost, neglected, or in deteriorating condition.

3. To promote and initiate new research in the field of Swedish-American studies.

4. To arrange, or assist in arranging, conferences of scholars and writers dealing with different aspects of Swedish immigration. Also to help preserve knowledge of the Swedish-American heritage through exhibits, lectures, and occasional publications.

5. To provide assistance to persons doing research in Swedish-American sources.

6. To facilitate both the preservation and dissemination of Swedish-American materials through microfilming, shared cataloging and indexing, and related projects.

7. To work closely with other organizations interested in Swedish-American studies, as well as to maintain contacts with similar organizations from other ethnic groups, thereby participating in and contributing to the study of the role of ethnicity in American life.

Activities   Archives, library, and research facilities occupy three levels in Denkmann Hall (the old College library) on the Augustana campus. A professional staff is employed to direct the programs of the Center and to assist those who wish to use its facilities. In 1988 the Center established the O. Fritiof Ander lectureship in immigration history, usually held in the spring of each year.

Publications SWENSON CENTER NEWS (since 1986), annual publication, free of charge; GUIDE TO RESOURCES AND HOLDINGS (rev. ed., 1989; 1991 update in progress), free of charge; Marcus Lee Hansen, THE PROBLEM OF THE THIRD   GENERATION IMMIGRANT (a republication of the 1937 address with new introductions, 1987), $2.00 per copy; distributed through the Center is SWEDISH-AMERICAN NEWSPAPERS: A GUIDE TO THE MICROFILMS HELD BY THE SWENSON SWEDISH IMMIGRATION RESEARCH CENTER (1981), $1.00 per copy; available on microfiche are computerized listings of the Center's holdings of microfilmed Swedish-American and Swedish-Canadian church records, $1.00 per set.

◆ Texas Swedish Cultural Foundation, Inc.

c/o Birger Jansson
8211 S. Braeswood
Houston, TX 77071
Tel. (713)771-8168

President   Birger Jansson

Founded   1951

Trustees   10

Purpose   The purpose of the Foundation is to promote good will
and cultural exchange between Sweden and Texas. The Foundation
sets up scholarships for exchange students between Sweden and
Texas in all fields of science, industry, and art.

Activities   The Foundation helps sponsor, promote, organize, and
fund Swedish cultural events, distributes literature on Sweden, and
sponsors the printing of information.

Publications A BIBLIOMANIAC ON THE TEXAS FRONTIER: SWANTE
PALM AND HIS SWEDISH LIBRARARY AND THE UNIVERSITY OF
TEXAS AT AUSTIN by Siv Vedung.

Texas Swedish Pioneer Association, Inc.

c/o Bert Magnuson
1200B Inland Greens
Austin, TX 78758
Tel. (512)835-5664

President   Bert Magnuson

Founded   Organized around 1900 by pioneers from Sweden
who arrived in 1867; incorporated in 1937.

Members   Number not given; membership restricted to persons
of pioneer Swedish ancestry.

Purpose   To promote and preserve the Swedish heritage of the
immigrants who came to Texas in 1838 and the larger group in 1867.

Activities   Sponsor scholarships; help in restoring Swante Palm's grave, a Swedish blacksmith shop and a log cabin filled with Swedish relics; they are translating from Swedish to English, SVENSKARNA I TEXAS, first published in 1918; they meet on the last Sunday in June each year.

Affiliate

Austin Scandinavian Club

◆ Three Crowns American Swedish Association

c/o Quentin Paulson
7051 University Drive
Bismarck, ND 58504
Tel. (701)222-1519

President   Quentin Paulson

Founded   1980

Members   87

Purpose   To promote interest and understanding of the Swedish heritage and culture and to promote fellowship among the members and friendship between the United States and Sweden.

Activities   a Julotta Christmas service; a St. Lucia Day celebration; Midsummer picnic; movies; lectures; programs on genealogy; language study; food preparation; sponsoring Swedish musical groups and dances.

Publication   A newsletter.

◆ Tre Kronor Scandinavian Society

c/o Mrs. Louis Titus
806 East Avenue
Holdrege, NE 68949
Tel. (308)995-8567

President   Mrs. Louis Titus

Founded   April 1989

Members   112

Purpose   To further their knowledge of their Scandinavian heritage and to promote this to the community, especially to the young people.

Activities   Assisting the Chamber of Commerce with the Swedish Days celebration; helping crown a Swedish King and Queen every year; helping dedicate the restored Swedish church; working with the museum and restored Swedish church on events; A Swedish Midsummer; genealogy research for members families; education; sponsoring programs.

Twin Cities Swedish Folk Dancers

c/o Jim & Lorraine McGrath
542 E. Idaho Avenue
St. Paul, MN 55101
Tel. (612)771-6780

Instructor   Jim McGrath

Coordinator Lorraine McGrath

Founded   1918

Members   22

Purpose   To preserve and promote ethnic Swedish folk dancing through teaching and performances.

Activities   The members engage in folk dance practices and performances.

Twin City Dalaförening

c/o Gunhild Anderson
3912 Minnehaha Avenue, Apt. 1
Minneapolis, MN 55406
Tel. (612)729-4905

President   Gunhild Anderson

Founded   1947

Members   100

Purpose   The group's purpose is to meet with people from the province of Dalarna and to enjoy and preserve the songs, dances, and culture from Dalarna.

Activities   The members hold social events with singing and dancing, an annual dinner, summer picnic, and Christmas party.

◆ United Swedish Societies (Svenska Centralförbundet)

20 Bristol Avenue
Staten Island, NY 10301
Tel. (718)442-1096
Fax (718)442-5376

President   Harry V. Hedin

Founded   1903

Members   35 member organizations

Purpose   The United Swedish Societies of New York is an umbrella organization for Swedish-American organizations in the metropolitan New York area. The organization's purpose is to achieve closer cooperation among Swedish societies in New York city and its surrounding areas in questions and matters which may be of common interest and advantage.

Activities   An annual Sweden Day at Midsummer; bazaar for fundraising; seasonal and special Swedish ethnic celebrations.

Vasa Nordic Club

Viola Landholm
Rt. 3, Box 230
Wausa, NE 68786

President   Gene Johnson

Founded   1988

Members   35

Purpose   To promote and preserve our Scandinavian heritage and traditions.

Activities   An annual crowning of a Midsummer Day Queen.

◆ Vasa Order of America

c/o Gladys Birtwistle
65 Bryant Road
Cranston, RI 02910
Tel. (401)461-0016

**Grand
Master**   George A. Nord

Founded   1896

Members   31,000

Purpose   The purpose of the Vasa Order of America, a Swedish American fraternal organization, is to promote and perpetuate the Swedish traditions and culture in America.

Activities   The organization's 326 lodges throughout the United States, Canada, and Sweden conduct a variety of educational and group activities which include language, craft, history and culture classes, musical theatrical and folk dancing activities, the sponsorship of various public events, and a scholarship program for high school students who are members of Vasa Order of America.

Publications THE VASA STAR (VASASTJÄRNAN), a monthly magazine received by all members. Newsletters are distributed by local lodges.

District Lodges

Connecticut District Lodge, No. 1
Dale Youngstrom, District Master
23 Chapman Road W.
Hartford, CT 06107
(203)521-0874

Massachusetts District Lodge, No. 2
Nancy Darling, District Master
34 Federal Hill Road
Auburn, MA 01501
(508)832-9020

Rhode Island District Lodge, No. 3
Robert Fraser, District Master
21 Benbridge Avenue
Warwick, RI 02888
(401)781-3655

New York District Lodge, No. 4
Theodore Fredrickson, District Master
151 Berkshire Drive
Rochester, NY 14626
(716)225-8409

New Jersey District Lodge, No. 6
Paul H. Thenstedt, District Master
1929 Cloverdale Road
Bethlehem, PA 18018
(215)691-2296

Minnesota District Lodge, No. 7
Nancy A. Bayle, District Master
540 Highway 61 East
Two Harbors, MN 55616
(218)834-2998

Illinois District Lodge, No. 8
John Weber, District Master
21129 E. Glen Haven Circle
Northville, MI 48167
(313)348-5594

Pennsylvania District Lodge, No. 9
Rolf Bergman, District Master
3236 Berkeley
Cleveland Heights, OH 44118
(216)371-5141

Superior, Michigan and Wisconsin District Lodge, No. 10
William H. Kueck, Jr., District Master
N269 River Drive
Menominee, MI 49858
(906)863-6052

Rocky Mountain District Lodge, No. 11
Charles Wood, District Master
5562 S. Jamaica Way
Englewood, CO 80111

Golden Gate District Lodge, No. 12
Helen Mingram, District Master
6752 Harrisburg Place
Stockton, CA 95207
(209)951-3260

Pacific Northwest District Lodge, No. 13
Leslie N. Ostlund, District Master
1657 Meadowlark Drive NE
Salem, OR 97303
(503)393-3297

Pacific Southwest District Lodge, No. 15
Harvey B. Peterson, District Master
17600 Lahey Street
Granada Hills, CA 91344
(818)360-1654

Central Canada District Lodge, No. 16
Verna Lundin, District Master
640 6th Avenue S.
Kenora, ON P9N 2C6 Canada
(807)468-6326

Iowa-Nebraska District Lodge, No. 17
Harold Olsen, District Master
4554 Poppleton Avenue
Omaha, NE 68106
(402)551-7305

Alberta District Lodge, No. 18
Ray Nyroos, District Master
7207 92 B Avenue
Edmonton, AB T6B 0W3 Canada
(403)469-0259

Sweden Distriktlogen, Nr. 19, Norra Sverige
Aldor Jansson, Distriktmästare
Grev Turegatan 62, 4tr.
S-114 38 Stockholm, Sweden
011 46 8 66 29 638

Sweden Distriktlogen, Nr. 20, Södra Sverige
Lars Helgeson, Distriktmästare
Skånegatan 15
S-216 11 Malmö, Sweden
011 46 8 40 15 78 57

Arizona District Lodge, No. 21
Pat Flippen, District Master
1875 Paradise Lane
Prescott, AZ 86301
(602)778-9333

Vasa Order of America Youth Clubs

Connecticut District No. 1
Sandra Newell
10 Vineyard Road
Branford, CT 06405

Massachusetts District No. 2
Anna Mae Marron
24 Elm Shade Way Boston Road Trailer Park
Springfield, MA 01119

Rhode Island District No. 3
Kristina Greiner
449 Narragansett Parkway
Warwick, RI 02888

New York District No. 4
Marie-Louise Olson
1A Richard Place
Lake Ronkonkoma, NY 11779

New Jersey District No. 6
Carole L. Anderson
12 Brookside Avenue
Basking Ridge, NJ 07010

Minnesota District No. 7
Janice Lehman
3109 32nd Avenue S.
Minneapolis, MN 55406

Illinois District No. 8
Diane Overby
5142 N. Lowell
Chicago, IL 60620

Pennsylvania District No. 9
Viola Hjelm
1414 E. Miner Road
Mayfield Heights, OH 44121

Golden Gate District No. 12
Florence Griffith
2144 Inman Avenue
Stockton, CA 95204

Pacific Northwest District No. 13
Judy Rust
10835 N.E. Fremont
Portland, OR 97220

Pacific Southwest District No. 15
Birgitta Roodsari
1640 Ivy Bridge
Glendale, CA 91207

Alberta Canada District No. 18
Carol Banks
11 Lloyd Place
St. Albert, AB T8N 2H4
CANADA

Norra Sverige Distrikt Nr. 19
Berith Blomgren
Sighultsvägen 23
S-451 34 Uddevalla
SWEDEN

Södra Sverige Distrikt Nr. 20
Ulla Roos
Västerängsvägen 4
S-393 53 Kalmar
SWEDEN

Archives   Information regarding the Vasa Order of America, Inc. may be obtained by contacting the following individual:

Bertil G. Winstrom
4720 W. Parkview Drive
Mequon, WI 53092
(414)242-2973

◆ Vasa Order of America - Carl Larsson Lodge #739

c/o Ruth Gustafson Allinger
1920 Hillock Drive
Raleigh, NC 27612
Tel. (919)787-2505

Chairman   Rita Hollinghurst

Founded   April 26, 1986

Members   100

Purpose   The Carl Larsson Lodge is part of Vasa Order of America, a Swedish-American fraternal organization, originally started to provide sick and death benefits. Today the emphasis is on the moral, intellectual, and social development of Scandinavian, and involvement of younger generations in the culture and traditions.

Activities   Monthly programs coordinated with traditional Swedish foods eaten at that time (e.g. Sept. -crayfish, Nov. - Mårtengås dinner, etc.); dinner dance with accordionist Walter Eriksson; celebration of King Carl XVI Gustaf's birthday; a St. Lucia pageant; Julbord; Midsummer celebration with dancing around the maypole.

Publication   C.L. POSTEN, a monthly newsletter.

◆ Vasa Order of America - Drott Lodge #168

c/o Richard Sanders, Recording Secretary
10243 Arizona Circle
Bethesda, MD 20817
Tel. (301)365-4658

Chairman   Dave Johnson

Founded   1910

Members   270

Purpose   To promote and preserve Swedish culture and traditions, and to educate our members in the same.

Activities   Swedish bazaar; St. Lucia pageant; Midsummer picnic; presentations of Swedish music; lectures on Swedish or Swedish-American culture, history, immigration, arts, crafts, architecture; lectures by Swedish Embassy staff; films; slide shows.

Publication   DROTTS NYHETER, a monthly newsletter.

◆ Vasa Order of America - Svea Lodge #253

c/o Raye Wilkinson
4533 Mimi Drive
Indianapolis, IN 46237
Tel. (317)784-9418

President   Dan Anderson

Founded   May 29, 1913

Members   161

Purpose   To represent the Scandinavian community of central Indiana and to promote social and intellectual activities among its members; to teach and preserve the Swedish language; to promote the culture and heritage of the Scandinavian people; and to maintain contacts with the Scandinavian countries and their people.

Activities   Kräftskiva; St. Lucia; Midsummer; participation in the Indianapolis International Festival.

Publication   A monthly newsletter.

◆ Vasa Order of America - Valhalla Lodge #715

c/o E. Bernice Belzone, Secretary
3150 S. Arville, #1
Las Vegas, NV 89102
Tel. (702)362-7240

President   Carl Jarnberg

Founded   November 15, 1975

Members   61

Purpose   To preserve and promote Scandinavian culture and heritage by providing activities for both Scandinavians residing in America and Americans interested in Scandinavia.

Activities   Ten monthly business/social meetings per year, along with several celebrations, i.e. St. Lucia Christmas party; Midsummer picnic; Lodge's anniversary dinner party; and the International Food Festival.

Publications Newsletters and bulletins sent to members during the year.

◆ Vasa Order of America - Viking Lodge #730

c/o Lilli Jalbing
8517 Arbela Road
Millington, MI 48746
Tel. (517)871-3467

President   Bill Lundquist

Founded   May 15, 1981

Purpose   To maintain and teach traditions, culture, heritage, and language and to promote opportunities to inform and maintain these purposes.

Activities   Traditional Christmas; St. Lucia and Midsummer programs; monthly meetings, except July and August, in addition to special observances.

Publications Monthly information letter for members; VALT-HORNET, a quarterly district newsletter; THE VASA STAR, a monthly international publication

Viking Age Club

c/o Dennis Rusinko
617 24th Avenue N.E.
Minneapolis, MN 55418
Tel. (612)789-2272

President   Viki Reyburn

Founded   1985

Members   30

Purpose   A non-profit corporation to promote the study and re-creation of everyday life in the Viking Age.

Activities   Monthly meetings (call contact person for specific dates and sites); the club has participated in local Scandinavian festivals as well as the Swedish Festival in Oakland, Nebraska, the Norwegian festival in Decorah, Iowa, the Norsk Høstfest in Minot, North Dakota, Duluth's Viking Festival in Duluth, Minnesota, and the Hjemkomst Heritage Days in Moorhead, Minnesota.

Publication   A newsletter.

Vikingland American Scandinavian Organization

Elda Lindquist, Vice President
Route 3, Lake Mina
Alexandria, MN 56308

President   Ray Englund

Founded   1980

Members   100-150

Purpose   Mostly social.

Activities   A smörgåsbord at Christmas time; a Walpurgis celebration in April; a Midsummer celebration in June; a Swedish language class.

Värmlandsförbundet of Minnesota

c/o Delores A. Meyers
8624 W. 35th Street
St. Louis Park, MN 55426
Tel. (612)938-2666

Chairman Delores A. Meyers

Founded 1927

Members 125

Purpose To preserve Swedish heritage and in particular to maintain significant connections with Värmland, and to provide the opportunity for those with these interests to socialize.

Activities The organization sponsors social activities as well as tours and exhibits. Monthly meetings are held September through May on the 3rd Saturday of each month.

◆ Värmlands Vännerna

c/o Alvalene Karlsson
1457 Third Avenue
New York, NY 10028
Tel. (212)744-8224

President Alvalene Karlsson

Founded 1971

Members 35

Purpose To preserve the culture of Värmland in the United States and to support the Emigrant Register in Karlstad, Sweden.

Activities Guest speakers; musical presentations; attendance in costume at Swedish-American events.

◆ West Shore Scandinavian Society

c/o Lois Soneral
501 Sixth Street
Ludington, MI 49431
Tel. (616)843-8153

President Dorothy Engwall

Founded 1982

Members 75

Purpose   To preserve, promote, and publicize the culture, heritage, and traditions of the Scandinavian countries; to provide the membership and the general public of the West Shore area with opportunities to know and enjoy such culture, heritage, and traditions; to provide fellowship among the members.

Activities   Sponsorship of Scandinavian exchange musical and dance groups; providing Christmas decorations for historical museum display in Ludington and Manistee, Michigan; establishing a fund to donate Scandinavian books to West Shore Community College; and hosting a Scandinavian costume workshop.

Publication   SCANDI-NEWS, a newsletter.

◆ Western Carolinas Association of ASF

c/o Eiler R. Cook
PO Box 2296
Hendersonville, NC 28793
Tel. (704)692-0323

President   Eiler R. Cook

Founded   March 1982

Members   100

Purpose   An affiliate of the American Scandinavian Foundation, it promotes cultural exchange and understanding between the United States and the five Nordic nations.

Activities   Scandinavian bazaar every November; St. Lucia festival and First Advent Scandinavian service; guest speaker from one of the Nordic embassies every February; social gatherings with various themes (i.e. Midsummer, Norwegian May 17th, Swedish pea soup dinner, summer operetta, picnics, etc.); selected charitable contributions; making Scandinavian books and periodicals available to area universities, colleges, and libraries.

Publication   A periodic newsletter.

Ölandsklubben

c/o Thyra Johnson
4 John Street
Shoreham, NY 11786
Tel. (516)744-8842

President   Oddvar Skadberg

Founded   1928

Members   35

Purpose   To bring together people from Öland now living in the New York area; to meet and exchange memories, as well as to assist each other in sickness and distress.

Activities   Social.

.

Swedish organizations that promote contact with the United States

A number of agencies and organizations in Sweden play an important role in relations with the United States. These organizations disseminate information, sponsor exchanges of students and scholars, and provide contact between Americans living in Sweden and Swedes. In some instances, an organization or agency includes Swedish-American relations as part of a broader program of contact between Sweden and other countries.

American Club of Sweden

PO Box 16346
S-103 26 Stockholm
SWEDEN
Tel. 011 46 8 10 56 82

President   Michael Hammarskjöld

Purpose   The present club is the result of a merger in 1980 of the American Club of Stockholm and the Swedish-American Society of Stockholm. Its purpose is to work for the strengthening of bonds between the U.S. and Sweden by interchange of knowledge, customs, and ideals through social gatherings among its members and guests.

Activities   The American Club of Sweden plays an important role as an informal point of contact between the various elements of the Swedish-American community and provides frequent opportunities for interaction through its monthly luncheons with lectures and guest speakers and various social programs usually highlighted by the annual Thanksgiving Day dinner dance and the 4th of July celebration.

The Commission for Educational Exchange between the United States and Sweden

(The Fulbright Commission)

Nämnden för svensk-amerikanskt forskarutbyte
(Fulbrightkommissionen)
Vasagatan 15-17
S-111 20 Stockholm
SWEDEN
Tel. 011 46 8 10 64 50
011 46 8 10 65 15
Fax 011 46 8 14 10 64

Director   Jeannette Lindström

Purpose   The purpose of the Commission is to promote mutual understanding between the people of the United States and Sweden through academic exchanges and by supporting programs of American Studies at Swedish universities and Swedish Studies at American universities. The Commission has a board consisting of four American members appointed by the American Ambassador to Sweden and four Swedish members appointed by the Swedish Ministry for Foreign Affairs. The Commission is funded by the Swedish and American governments.

Activities   The Commission awards grants to American and Swedish graduate students and postdoctoral scholars to study, teach, or conduct research in Sweden or the United States. The Commission also provides information about studying in the United States.

◆ The Emigrant Register in Karlstad

Emigrantregistret
Södra Kyrkogatan 4
S-651 08 Karlstad
SWEDEN
Tel. 011 46 54 15 92 69
011 46 54 15 92 72
Fax 011 46 54 18 90 77

Governor   Ingemar Eliasson

Director   Erik Gustavson

Purpose   The Emigrant Register was founded in 1960 by the Värmland Historical Society and the Karlstad Lodge of the Vasa Order of America. Its purpose is to investigate the family connections, origin, and places of residence of the emigrants from Sweden to American and their descendants as well as to strengthen the bonds between the descendants of Swedish emigrants and their kinfolk in Sweden. Files on the emigrants from Sweden to American, which have been collected by the Emigrant Register, include the writings of emigrants in the form of diaries, letters, and memoirs; publicity, correspondence, and receipts of travel agencies; files of both Swedish and Swedish-American newspapers and magazines; and books.

Activities   Comprehensive studies regarding emigration are carried out in close cooperation with the Department of American History at the University of Uppsala. The Emigrant Register assists visitors in their search for information about relatives. The Emigrant Register also arranges the John Ericsson Day each summer.

Affiliate   The Society for the Promoting of Emigration Research
Samfundet Emigrantforskningens Främjande

The Society was founded in 1969 to support the activities of the Emigrant Register. The Society publishes the quarterly *Bryggan - The Bridge* which since 1972 is distributed in both a Swedish and an English edition.

Chairman Per-Erik Nordquist

◆ The National Association for Contact with Sweden

Riksföreningen Sverigekontakt
Dicksonsgatan 6
Box 53066
S-400 14 Göteborg
SWEDEN
Tel. 011 46 31 18 00 62
Fax   011 46 31 20 99 02

Secretary
General   Lennart Limberg

Purpose   The purpose of the Association, which was founded in 1908, is to promote worldwide contact between Sweden and its citizens and their descendants and to provide Swedish citizens in foreign countries with information about Swedish culture, the Swedish language, and Swedish social conditions. The organization has local chapters in Sweden and Finland and a sister organization in the United States, the Swedish Cultural Society in America.

Publication SVERIGEKONTAKT

Radio Sweden
Riksradions utlandsprogram
S-105 10 Stockholm
SWEDEN
Tel. 011 46 8 784 00 00
Fax 011 46 8 667 62 83

Director Hans Wachholz

Address in the United States
Swedish Broadcasting Company
12 West 37th Street, 7th floor
New York, NY 10018-7404
Fax (212)594-6413

Representative Elisabeth Johansson

Activities Radio Sweden provides daily worldwide broadcasts in Swedish, English, French, German, Spanish, Estonian, Latvian, and Russian. The broadcasts include Swedish, Scandinavian and international news, commentaries, interviews, and overviews of current topics, Swedish music, etc. Programs with informative, documentary content, and program series with Swedish music are available to foreign radio stations.

The Sweden-America Foundation
Sverige-Amerika Stiftelsen
Grev Turegatan 14
Box 5280
S-102 46 Stockholm
SWEDEN
Tel. 011 46 8 611 46 11 or 011 46 8 611 46 44

Director Lillemor Mundebo

Purpose The Foundation was founded in 1919 and is supported by representatives of private business, industry, and organizations. Its purpose is to further relations between Sweden and the United States and Canada by promoting the exchange of scientific, cultural, and practical information, mainly by means of fellowships awarded to qualified young Swedish men and women for research and study in the United States. The Foundation cooperates with the American-Scandinavian Foundation (725 Park Avenue, New York, NY 10021) and with the Institute of International Education (809 United Nations Plaza, New York, NY 10017) and others.

◆ The Swedish Emigrant Institute (SEI)

Svenska Emigrantinstitutet
Box 201
S-351 04 Växjö
SWEDEN
Tel. 011 46 470 201 20
Fax 011 46 470 394 16

Director   Ulf Beijbom

Purpose   Founded in 1965, the Swedish Emigrant Institute is a private foundation supported by the State and the local communities of Växjö and Kronoberg County. The Institute's purpose is:

1. To work for intensified contact between descendants in America of emigrants from Sweden and the country of their ancestors.

2. To develop and further knowledge about the Swedish emigration, especially the emigration to the United States.

3. To establish libraries, archives, and exhibitions for this purpose with material illustrating the history of emigration.

4. To support scholarly and lay research in this field.

Activities   The Swedish Emigrant Institute collects material on Swedish emigrants and emigration from all over the world. Most of the material, however, relates to the emigration to the United States and Canada. The registers, indexes, and excerpt collections are the largest of their kind with over two million register cards. The Institute's library contains Sweden's largest book collection on emigrants and emigration. The House of Emigrants offers a variety of exhibitions open from 9 am to 4 pm on weekdays, 11 am to 3 pm on Saturday, and 1 pm to 5 pm on Sunday. The Institute sponsors

The Swedish Emigrant Institute in Växjö.

lectures, exhibits, and conferences on different topics relating to Swedish emigration. The Institute also acts as a service institution for historians and family researchers with the research room open on weekdays from 9 am to 4 pm.

The Swedish Institute

Hamngatan 27
Box 7434
S-103 91 Stockholm
SWEDEN
Tel. 011 46 8 789 20 00
Fax 011 46 8 20 72 48

Director   Anders Clason

Information about Sweden Ove Svensson

Cultural Exchange   Sonja Martinson-Uppman

Studies and Research   Thomas Lundén

Administration   Mats Backström

Purpose   The Swedish Institute (SI) is a government-financed foundation established to:

- disseminate knowledge abroad about Swedish society and culture by means of information activities

- promote cultural and informational exchange between Sweden and other countries

- promote educational and research exchange between Sweden and other countries

- promote the teaching of Swedish as a foreign language abroad

- manage the activities of the Swedish Cultural Centre in Paris (Centre culturel suédois, CCS).

The Institute's activities form part of Sweden's participation in the international cultural, educational, research, and informational exchanges and are thus aimed at bringing about an exchange of experiences, ideas, knowledge, and cultural manifestations. This exchange gives both Sweden and its partner countries additional opportunities of benefiting from each other's knowledge and experiences. The Institute's work in the fields of general information, interchange of experience, and culture, moreover, helps to increase knowledge abroad of Swedish social life and cultural patterns and to generate understanding for Swedish opinions and values.

Another of the Institute's important concerns is to advise institutions and individual persons on matters relating to international exchange. The Swedish Institute is managed by a board appointed by the Government and represents the Ministry for Foreign Affairs, the Ministry of Education and Cultural Affairs, cultural life, the education system, the popular movements, the trade union movements, mass media, and industry.

The Swedish International Press Bureau

Svenska Internationella Pressbyrån, SIP
PO Box 5529
S-114 85 Stockholm
SWEDEN
Tel. 011 46 8 783 80 00
Fax 011 46 8 661 48 07

Publisher   Lars-Erik Lingström

Purpose   The Bureau was founded in 1927 and since 1938 has been affiliated with the General Export Association of Sweden. It is a private organization, but it is financed jointly by private enterprise and the government.

The Swedish International Press Bureau supplies news media throughout the world with news reports on Swedish developments in various fields, with emphasis on economy, commerce, and industry as well as science, technology, and the social sciences. A picture service is also available to supplement the textual material.

The material is distributed in seven languages (English, German, French, Spanish, Dutch, Japanese, and Portuguese) either directly from Stockholm or through representatives abroad. The Bureau works in close cooperation with the Swedish Foreign Service which in several countries distributes the material locally to the press, the authorities, and organizations.

◆ Södra Vätterbygdens Folkhögskola

c/o Hans Nilsson
Fjällgatan 16
S-554 39 Jönköping
SWEDEN
Tel. 011 46 36 16 50 25

President   Kerstin Thornborg

Founded   1921

Purpose   To give Swedish students possibilities to study in the
United States and American students possibilities to study in Sweden.

Activities   Yearly exchange programs.

Publication SVF-NYTT, a newsletter.

EDUCATIONAL
ORGANIZATIONS

♦ Augustana College

Rock Island, IL 61201
Tel. (309)794-7000

Officers of Administration

Thomas Tredway, President
Arne Selbyg, Dean of the College
Glen E. Brolander, Vice President for Financial Affairs and
    Treasurer
John L. Kindschuh, Vice President for Planning and Advance-
    ment
John W. Hullett, Dean of Enrollment Management

Enrollment   2,214 full-time, 39 part-time

Augustana is a liberal arts college which is related to the Evangelical
Lutheran Church in America. The College traces its origin to the universities of Uppsala and Lund in Sweden. Graduates of these ancient European seats of learning founded Augustana in 1860 on the near north side
of Chicago.

Augustana College and Theological Seminary, as it was first known,
moved from Chicago to Paxton, Illinois, in 1863, and finally to Rock
Island in 1875. The Seminary became a separate institution in 1948 and
in 1967 returned to Chicago as part of the Lutheran School of Theology.

Augustana is accredited by the North Central Association of Colleges
and Secondary Schools, the National Association of Schools of Music, the
National Council for the Accreditation of Teacher Education, and the
American Chemical Society. Since 1948 the College has had a chapter of
Phi Beta Kappa.

Augustana is located in Rock Island, one of several cities in the
complex known as the Quad Cities.

Concentrated study in a major field within the humanities, the
natural or social sciences, or in one of the fields of professional preparation
offered at Augustana is required of each student. The College's commitment to the liberal arts is expressed in its general graduation requirements.
Each student is asked to study in a broad range of fields, including writing,
literature, foreign languages, fine arts, philosophy, religion, social science,
natural science, and physical education.

The College's size and character foster personal contact between
students and faculty, both in and outside of formal academic situations.
Augustana encourages the personal as well as the academic growth of its
students through a full range of co- and extra-curricular activities.

The Swedish heritage continues to be identified in many areas of the
College's program. Special scholarships are available for students of
Swedish descent. A major in Scandinavian offers opportunities for con-
centrated study of the Swedish language and Scandinavian literature.
Majors in Scandinavian, economics, geography, history, or political

science may add specialization in Scandinavian Area Studies by taking approved courses in Scandinavian culture. Each year a summer school in Sweden provides the opportunity for intensive language study, and each year students are exchanged with the Universities of Uppsala and Karlstad.

The Augustana College Library has the largest holdings in the United States of Swedish-American newsprint and periodicals, and the most important manuscript collection of Swedish Lutheran pioneer leaders in America. The Swenson Swedish Immigration Research Center offers unusual opportunities for the study of Swedish-American history. The Augustana Historical Society is associated with the College.

The David M. Loring Map Library contains a large number of maps covering the Scandinavian countries. It includes maps of historic value as well as contemporary cultural and topographic maps.

◆ Bethany College

Lindsborg, KS 67456
Tel. (913)227-3311

Officers of Administration

Joel M. McKean, President
Richard Torgerson, Vice President and Academic Dean
Louise Cummings-Simmons, Director of Admissions and Financial Aid
Bill Wade, Director of Institutional Advancement
A. John Pearson, Director of College Relations

Enrollment   700

Bethany is a college of liberal arts which is dedicated to a program of Christian higher education. A college of the Evangelical Lutheran Church in America, Bethany is supported directly by the Missouri-Kansas, Arkansas-Oklahoma, and Rocky Mountain synods of the E.L.C.A.

The Rev. Dr. Carl Aaron Swensson, a Lutheran pastor and educator, founded Bethany College in 1881 in Lindsborg in the heart of the Smoky

The Messiah Festival at Bethany College.

Valley region of central Kansas. The college was first known as an academy and in 1886 became Bethany College, graduating its first baccalaureate class in 1891.

Bethany College is accredited by the North Central Association of Colleges and Secondary Schools, the National Association of Schools of Music, the National Council for Accreditation of Teacher Education, and the Council for Social Work Education. Bethany College is on the American Association of University Women's qualified list.

Bethany provides courses of study in a broad spectrum of the liberal arts in a distinctive religious, cultural, and regional setting. In addition to the general academic program, Bethany is noted for special programs in music and art. The famed "Messiah" Festival has been held annually since 1882 during Holy Week. An extensive collection of the paintings of the well-known Swedish-American artist Birger Sandzén is located on the Bethany campus. Although the College seeks to serve primarily the enrolled students, it often hosts various groups, conferences, workshops, meetings, and cultural events, including ethnic Swedish-American activities.

Bethany College has a rich tradition and heritage extending back to the earliest immigrant pioneer days of the region. But the emphasis is on today. At Bethany are found many lively, forward-looking programs and campus activities. A great many new buildings and facilities have been constructed alongside some of the older ones. The campus now has a fresh, vibrant look, although the College community is very proud of its early Swedish-American and other historical heritage.

◆ Bethel College and Seminary

3900 Bethel Drive
St. Paul, MN 55112
Tel. (612)638-6230

Officers of Administration

George K. Brushaber, President
Millard J. Erickson, Executive Vice President and Dean of the Seminary
H. David Brandt, Provost of the College
Sherman A. Swenson, Executive Vice President for Administration and Finance
David A. Lissner, President, Bethel Foundation and Director of Campus Planning

Enrollment   1,815 in the College, 528 in the Seminary

Bethel College and Seminary is owned and operated by the Baptist General Conference of America.

In 1871, John Alexis Edgren founded a seminary for the education of Swedish immigrants in Chicago. At the turn of the century, Swedish

Baptists in Minneapolis began an academy offering high school vocational training.

In 1914, the seminary and academy were brought together on one campus in St. Paul, Minnesota. A junior college was added in 1931, both for general education and as a basis for theological studies. The academy was phased out and a four-year liberal arts college was established in 1947. Both the Seminary and the College are now located on a 231-acre campus in Arden Hills, a suburb of St. Paul.

Both the College and the Seminary are accredited by the North Central Association of Colleges and Secondary Schools. In addition, the Seminary is accredited by the American Association of Theological Schools. The college is also accredited by the National Council for Accreditation of Teacher Education and is certified by the State of Minnesota for elementary and secondary education programs, and it is registered with the Minnesota Higher Education Coordinating Board.

The Seminary offers five degrees: master of arts in theological studies, master of arts in Christian education, master of divinity, master of theology, and doctor of ministry.

The College offers the bachelor of arts, bachelor of science, bachelor of music, bachelor of music education, and associate of arts degrees. Students may choose from more than 70 fields of study within more than 60 majors. The academic program at Bethel College is enriched by its membership in programs of the Christian College Consortium, the Upper Midwest Association for Intercultural Education, and the Institute of Holy Land Studies.

A recent addition to the College program is Bethel's Program in Adult College Education (PACE). PACE is an adult degree completion program open to people 25 years of age or older, who have at least two years of college education. PACE offers degrees in organizational studies, business management, and nursing.

Through the years, the College has maintained its Swedish heritage and courses in Scandinavian culture and civilization are offered as well as instruction in the Swedish language.

◆ Gustavus Adolphus College

St. Peter, MN 56082
Tel. (507)933-7537

Officers of Administration

Axel D. Steuer, President
Richard Fuller, Dean of the College
Ken Westphal, Vice President for Finance and Business Affairs
Owen Sammelson, Vice President for Administration
Robert A. Peterson, Vice President for Development
Cecil Eckhoff, Vice President for Alumni Affairs

Enrollment   2,350

Gustavus Adolphus College is a liberal arts college affiliated with the Evangelical Lutheran Church in America. It was founded in 1862 by Eric Norelius in Red Wing, Minnesota, for the purpose of training pastors and teachers for Lutheran immigrants from Sweden. The following year the school was moved to East Union, Carver County, and given the name of St. Ansgar's Academy. In 1876, it was again moved, this time to its present location, and given the name Gustavus Adolphus College, after Sweden's hero king who died in 1632.

Gustavus Adolphus College is accredited by the North Central Association of Colleges and Secondary Schools, the American Chemical Society, the National Council for the Accreditation of Teacher Education, and the National League for Nursing. It also hosts the Eta chapter of Phi Beta Kappa, the nation's oldest and most prestigious academic honor society.

Gustavus Adolphus College is proud of its Swedish heritage. This pride is manifested through programs and visible memorials that portray Sweden's distinguished contributions to the world in art, science, literature, and general culture, and likewise convey the contributions of its Swedish immigrant founders.

Folke Bernadotte Memorial Library, with a capacity of 300,000 volumes and study stations for more than 1,000 students, was dedicated in 1972 by Her Royal Highness Princess Christina. The Bernadotte International Student Scholarship Program has sponsored most of the College's international students since 1950. Another memorial to Count Bernadotte, the annual Bernadotte Institutes on World Affairs, for fifteen years brought world leaders to the campus for discussion of current affairs. The Institutes led the College to establish a program in Peace Education which is considered a model in American education.

The Nobel Foundation, Stockholm, has authorized both the Alfred Nobel Hall of Science, dedicated in 1963, and the Nobel Conference, annual discussions of science-based issues with Nobel laureates typically among the discussants. The 27th Nobel Conference was held in 1991 with delegations from over 200 colleges, universities, and other institutions in attendance. The Russel and Rhoda Lund Nobel Endowment, established in 1978, assures a permanent base of support for this respected series.

Four years of Swedish language study are offered along with a Scandinavian Studies major. Formal exchange programs have been arranged with Karlstad University in Värmland and Växjö University in Småland. Summer study programs are also available at Lund, Stockholm, Gothenburg, and Dalarna.

The Jussi Bjorling Concert Hall honors the artistry of Swedish opera singer Jussi Bjorling. Other campus buildings honoring persons of Swedish heritage include the Arthur H. Anderson Social Science Center, the Edwin J. Vickner Language Hall, Edgar M. Carlson Administration Building, Inez Rundstrom Hall, the O.J. Johnson Student Union, and the Lund Center for Physical Education and Health.

◆ Jamestown Community College

c/o Laurie Livingston
525 Falconer Street
Jamestown, NY 14701
Tel. (716)655-5220

Office of Administration
Dr. Timothy G. Davis, President

Enrollment   1500 full and 1900 part-time

Jamestown Community College is a two-year college affiliated with the State University of New York serving primarily the residents of Chautauqua and Cattaraugus counties. Sponsored by the city of Jamestown, Jamestown Community College was founded in 1950. The majority of the population of Jamestown is of Swedish heritage.

Lutheran School of Theology at Chicago

1100 East 55th Street
Chicago, IL 60615-5199
(312)753-0700

Office of Administration
Dr. William E. Lesher, President
Dr. Ralph W. Klein, Dean

Enrollment   ca. 400

The Lutheran School of Theology at Chicago came into existence in 1962 as the result of the merger of four Lutheran seminaries. The oldest of the predecessor institutions was Augustana Theological Seminary in Rock Island, Illinois, founded in 1860 by Swedish immigrants. Others involved in the first stage of the merger were Chicago Lutheran Theological Seminary, Maywood, Illinois; Grand View Seminary, Des Moines, Iowa; and Suomi Theological Seminary, Hancock, Michigan. In 1967 Central Lutheran Theological Seminary of Fremont, Nebraska, and in 1983 Christ Seminary-Seminex, St. Louis, Missouri, were also merged with the consolidated seminary at Chicago.

The School is affiliated with the Evangelical Lutheran Church in America. In partnership with Wartburg Theological Seminary it sponsors the Lutheran Seminary Program in the Southwest, located in Austin, Texas. It works cooperatively with the Association of Chicago Theological

Schools and is accredited by the Association of Theological Schools in the United States and Canada, and the North Central Association of Colleges and Schools.

Located in the Hyde Park neighborhood of Chicago, Lutheran School of Theology at Chicago is a few blocks from the University of Chicago and five of the Chicago's 12 seminaries. The School offers special programs such as the Chicago Center for Religion and Science, the Center for Global Mission, the Hispanic Ministry Program, the Center for Public Ministry, and Rural Ministry.

Currently the following degrees are offered:
Master of Arts (M.A.)
Master of Divinity (M.Div.)
Master of Theology (Th.M.)
Doctor of Theology (Th.D.)
Doctor of Ministry (D.Min.)
Doctor of Ministry in Pastoral Care

Minnehaha Academy

3107 47th Avenue South
Minneapolis, MN 55406-2398
Tel. (612)729-8321

Officers of Administration
Craig W. Nelson, President
Kenneth D. Greener, Principal, North Campus
Dean C. Erickson, Principal, South Campus
Pam Johnson, Admissions Director

Enrollment   1,111 (Grades K-12)

Minnehaha Academy is owned and operated by the Northwest Covenant Conference of the Evangelical Covenant Church of America.

Following a decision in 1905 to organize Minnehaha Academy, property was purchased in South Minneapolis near the Mississippi River. The school opened in 1913.

The curriculum prepares students for college entrance; in addition, a strong music program and Bible department are offered. In all areas, Bible classes and chapel attendance are required.

The main building was erected in 1913. In 1922, an auditorium building was added; in 1949 an auditorium/gymnasium; and in 1977 a fine arts building.

In 1981, a 12 acre campus, 1 1/2 miles south of the original campus was purchased. A Middle School, grades 6-8, was established there. The Upper School remained at the North Campus. In August, 1982, a Lower School, grades 1-5, was opened on the South Campus; and in 1985, kindergarten was added to the offerings.

Minnehaha Academy sponsors a complete program of boys' and girls' interscholastic athletics as a member of the Tri-Metro Conference of the Minnesota State High School Program.

Accreditation is through the North Central Association of Schools and Colleges.

◆ North Park College and Theological Seminary

3225 West Foster Avenue
Chicago, IL 60625-4895
Tel. 312/583-2700

Officers of Administration

David G. Horner, President
Robert K. Johnston, Provost
I. Dean Ebner, Academic Dean of the College
Edward Eddy, Dean of Student Development for the College
Randy Tumblin, Director of College Admissions
Klyne Snodgrass, Dean of the Seminary Faculty
Anne Vining Pederson, Director of Seminary Admissions

Enrollment   College, 945; M.B.A. Graduate Program, 60;
Seminary, 135

North Park College and Theological Seminary was founded in 1891 by the Evangelical Covenant Church, a denomination made up of Swedish immigrants. Established in Minneapolis in 1891, the school moved to the North Side of Chicago in 1894.

Today, North Park is a four-year Christian liberal arts college and a graduate theological seminary. The college offers the B.A., B.S., and B.S. in medical technology degrees with 39 majors in the undergraduate program. In 1991 the college established its first graduate program, the M.B.A., with an ethics-across-the curriculum emphasis. Since 1989 the college has been named by *U.S. News & World Report* as one of the top 10 regional liberal arts colleges in the Midwest. The college is accredited by the North Central Association of Colleges and Secondary Schools.

The seminary offers three graduate degree programs including the master of divinity, master of arts in Christian education, and master of arts in theological studies. Housed in its own campus building, the seminary is accredited by the Association of Theological Schools.

The Center for Scandinavian Studies at North Park was chartered in 1984 to foster an understanding between Scandinavia and America. The Center sponsors programs emphasizing international business and economics, research and scholarship, and cultural exchanges. Each year a visiting Scandinavian scholar or lecturer-in-residence comes to the campus. North Park also maintains an exchange program with Södra

Vätterbydgens Folkhögskola in Jönköping, Sweden.

A lively interest in the history of Swedish immigrants and in American-Scandinavian cultural relations is evident on campus. The library includes a significant collection of books in Swedish and a special Jenny Lind collection. The campus also houses the archives of the Evangelical Covenant Church as well as those of the Swedish-American Historical Society.

Trinity College

2077 Half Day Road
Deerfield, IL 60015
Tel. (708)948-8980

Officers of Administration
Dr. Kenneth M. Meyer, President
Dr. Donna Peterson, Dean

Enrollment 900

Trinity Evangelical Divinity School

2065 Half Day Road
Deerfield, IL 60015
Tel. (708)945-8800

Officers of Administration
Dr. Kenneth M. Meyer, President
Dr. Walter C. Kaiser, Jr., Dean

Enrollment 1,400

The history of Trinity College and Trinity Evangelical Divinity School dates back to 1897 when members of the Swedish Evangelical Free Church of Chicago founded a Bible school in the basement of their church building. From that date, the Bible school was to take various forms, becoming in 1925 the Evangelical Free Church Seminary and Bible Institute of Chicago. Following its merger in 1946 with Trinity Seminary and Bible Institute of Minneapolis, a single college and seminary, Trinity Seminary and Bible College, emerged. In 1960, the Evangelical Free Church of America officially affirmed the college's four-year liberal arts program, while shortening its name to Trinity College, and a separate charter was granted to Trinity Seminary. In 1965 Trinity College moved to its present site in Deerfield, Illinois, where the seminary, previously named Trinity Evangelical Divinity School, had moved in 1961.

In 1974 the Annual Conference of the Evangelical Free Church of America voted to separate the college from the denomination. The Evangelical Free Church of America voted to re-affiliate with Trinity

College in 1983. Although today the seminary and college are separate units, there is a close cooperation and sharing of facilities and services between the two institutions.

Trinity College, fully accredited by the North Central Association of Colleges and Secondary Schools, features a four-year course of study leading to the bachelor of arts degree. The curriculum consists of the humanities, social sciences, and natural sciences and is distinctively Christian in its inclusion of Biblical studies as well as in its totally Christian perspective of teaching and learning.

In addition to its formal program, the college provides important intangibles essential for a full educational experience. Social and cultural events, varsity sports, Christian service activities, and small fellowship groups contribute to the educational needs of the students. Through its liberal arts program of general and pre-professional education, integrated with an evangelical commitment, Trinity College seeks to stimulate its students to full development intellectually, morally, socially, spiritually, and physically.

Trinity Evangelical Divinity School is a graduate theological school accredited by the Commission on Institutions of Higher Education of the North Central Association of Colleges and Secondary Schools and the Association of Theological Schools. The school is also a member of the Chicago Theological Institute, a consortium of five accredited theological schools in the north suburban area of metropolitan Chicago, and is affiliated with the Evangelical Free Church of America.

The purpose of the school is to educate men and women for a worldwide Christian ministry as pastors, missionaries, teachers, and lay leaders. Trinity Evangelical Divinity School emphasizes the comprehension of the Bible in its original languages, effective preaching, proficiency in the techniques of church administration, and effective missionary service. It seeks to prepare individuals for Christian ministry by leading its students to seek the truth through disciplined study and personal commitment and by providing its students with professional skills for the pastoral ministry and other closely related ministries of the church.

◆ Upsala College

East Orange, NJ 07019-1186
Tel. (201)266-7171

Officers of Administration

Robert E. Karsten, President
Warren Funk, Provost and Dean of the Faculty
Thomas L. Heaton, Vice President for Institutional Advancement
George Freyberger, Dean of Students
George Lynes, Dean of Admissions and Financial Aid Services

Enrollment   900

Upsala College is a small, private, liberal arts college. With a strong faculty and a quality academic program grounded in liberal learning, Upsala sets high academic expectations for its students.

Upsala was founded in 1893 by Swedish Lutherans as the fourth Swedish college in the United States and the first on the East Coast. Originally call the Upsala Institute of Learning, the College takes its name in honor of the 300th Anniversary of the historic Uppsala Decree, which officially established Uppsala University as the university of Sweden and the Lutheran Church as the church of Sweden.

Upsala's first homes were two Lutheran churches in Brooklyn, New York. In 1898, the College moved to a campus of its own in New Orange (now Kenilworth), New Jersey and was incorporated. In 1924, it moved to its present site in East Orange. The College also has an extension center, the Wirths Campus, in rural Sussex County, New Jersey.

The academic program of the College always has incorporated the study of liberal arts and sciences, although the early academic program required intensive English language and Swedish history studies. Today, Upsala offers baccalaureate degrees in 22 major fields in the humanities and natural sciences. The College also offers master of science degree programs in two areas. Students also may design their own interdisciplinary concentrations. Independent studies are available in all fields.

Upsala College is fully accredited by the Department of Higher Education of the State of New Jersey, the University of the State of New York, and the Middle States Association of Colleges and Secondary Schools.

Upsala's campus has excellent facilities for classroom work, athletic competition, and extracurricular activities. Located at the crossroads of New Jersey in East Orange, Upsala is just 15 miles from the educational, recreational, and cultural resources of New York City which students take advantage of regularly.

Instruction in Swedish Language and Culture

Instruction in Swedish language and culture is offered by a great number of institutions and organizations in the United States. Several major universities offer the M.A. and Ph.D. degrees in Scandinavian languages and literature; a number of universities and colleges offer the B.A. degree in Scandinavian (or Swedish) languages and literature and/or Scandinavian area programs. Individual courses in Swedish language and/or culture are offered in adult education programs in a great many universities and colleges as well as by various organizations.

The list that follows, arranged by state, is intended to provide an overview of the many institutions involved in Swedish studies in one form or another as well as addresses where further information may be obtained.

The *Directory of Scandinavian Studies in North America* edited by Robert B. Kvavik and published by the Society for the Advancement of Scandinavian Study (SASS) in 1989 gives a more comprehensive picture of the persons involved in Scandinavian teaching and research. The *Directory* may be ordered directly from SASS, c/o Professor Virpi Zuck, Department of Germanic Languages, University of Oregon, Eugene, OR 97403.

Instruction in Swedish Language and Culture:

Arizona

Swedish Educational Institute
Vasa Lodge
c/o Audrey Anderson
6802 N. Longfellow Dr.
Tucson, AZ 85718

California

University of California
Department of Scandinavian Studies
Berkeley, CA 94720

University of California
Department of German, Russian & Swedish
Davis, CA 95616

University of California
Department of Germanic Languages
Scandinavian Section
332 Royce Hall
405 Hilgard Avenue
Los Angeles, CA 90024

University of California
Department of Germanic, Oriental and Slavic Languages and
Literature
Santa Barbara, CA 93106

Stanford University
Department of Linguistics
Special Language Program
Stanford, CA 94305

Coastline Community College
2323 Placentia Avenue
Costa Mesa, CA 92626

Reseda Community Adult School
18230 Kittridge Street
Reseda, CA 91335

North Shores Community College
Adult Center
2455 Grand Avenue
San Diego, CA 92109

San Diego State University
Drama Department
San Diego, CA 92182

San Juan Unified School District
Winterstein Adult School
900 Morse Avenue
Sacramento, CA 95825

Santa Barbara Community College
Adult Education
Alice F. Schott Center
310 West Padre
Santa Barbara, CA 93105

Colorado

University of Colorado
Department of Germanic Languages and Literatures
McKenna 129
Campus Box 276
Boulder, CO 80309-0276

Denver University
The New College
University Park
Denver, CO 80208-0295

Connecticut

Yale University
Department of Germanic Languages and Literature
107 W.L. Harkness Hall
P.O. Box 18-A/Yale Station
New Haven, CT 06520

West Hartford Public Schools
Continuing Education Program
211 Steele Road
West Hartford, CT 06117

District of Columbia

U.S. Department of State
Foreign Service Institute
School of Language Studies SA-15
Swedish Section
Washington, DC 20007

Svenska skolan i Washington
Vuxenavdelningen
c/o Swedish Embassy
600 New Hampshire Avenue, N.W.
Washington, DC 20037

Florida

University of Florida
Department of Germanic and Slavic Languages and Literatures
263 Arts and Sciences Building
Gainesville, FL 32611

Illinois

North Park College
Swedish Department
3225 West Foster Avenue
Chicago, IL 60625-4987

Augustana College
Department of Scandinavian Studies
639 38th Street
Rock Island, IL 61201

University of Illinois
Department of Germanic Languages and Literatures
3072 Foreign Languages Building
707 South Mathews Avenue
Urbana-Champaign, IL 61801

Iowa

Augustana Lutheran Church
6th Court
Sioux City, IA 51101

Kansas

Heartland Learning Connection
P.O. Box 216
Maize, KS 67101

Kentucky

University of Kentucky
Department of Germanic Languages and Literatures
1055 Patterson Office Tower
Lexington, KY 40506

Maine

University of Southern Maine
Department of Community Programs
68 High Street
Portland, ME 04101

Maryland

University of Maryland
Department of Germanic and Slavic Languages and Literatures
Jimenez Hall
College Park, MD 20742

Massachusetts

University of Massachusetts
Department of Germanic Languages and Literatures
Herter Hall
Amherst, MA 01003

Harvard University
Department of Germanic Languages and Literature
421 Boylston Hall
Cambridge, MA 02138

Cambridge Center for Adult Education
42 Brattle Street
Cambridge, MA 02138

Michigan

University of Michigan
Department of Germanic Languages and Literature
3110 Modern Language Building
Ann Arbor, MI 48109

Ishpeming-Negaunee-Nice Community Schools
101 Pioneer Street
Negaunee, MI 49866

Minnesota

Mankato State University
Department of Scandinavian Studies
Mankato, MN 56001

The American Swedish Institute
2600 Park Avenue
Minneapolis, MN 55407

University of Minnesota
Institute of International Studies
208 Cina Hall
10 University Drive
Duluth, MN 55812-2496

University of Minnesota
Scandinavian Department
210 A Folwell Hall
Minneapolis, MN 55455

Moorhead State University
Department of Foreign Languages
P.O. Box 249
Moorhead, MN 56560

Gustavus Adolphus College
Department of Scandinavian Studies
St. Peter, MN 56082

Anoka-Hennepin School District II
Jackson Community Education
6000 109th Avenue North
Champlin, MN 55316

Eagle Bend High School
Eagle Bend, MN 56446

Chisago Lakes Area Senior High School and Community Education for Adults
Lindstrom, MN 55045

International Institute of Minnesota
1694 Como Avenue
St. Paul, MN 55108

New York

Cornell University
Department of Modern Languages and Linguistics
309 Morrill Hall
Ithaca, NY 14853

New York State University
Germanic and Slavic Department
Stony Brook, NY 11794

Jamestown Community College
525 Falconer Street
Jamestown, NY 14701

Church of Sweden
5 East 48th Street
New York, NY 10024

United Nations International School
24-50 East River Drive
New York, NY 10010

Vasa Order of America
Göta Lejon Lodge No. 84
A-12 Cedar Lane Apartments
Ossining, NY 10562

Vassar College
P.O. Box 20
Poughkeepsie, NY 12601

North Dakota

Svenska Vänner
3 Riverview Lane
Jamestown, ND 58401

Ohio

University of Cincinnati
Department of Germanic Languages and Literature
Old Chem 730-742
Mail location #372
Cincinnati, OH 45221

Ohio State University
Department of German
314 Cunz Hall of Languages
1841 Millikin Road
Columbus, OH 43210-1229

Oklahoma

The American-Scandinavian Culture Interest Group
P.O. Box 2189
Norman, OK 73070

Phillips University
International Studies Program
P.O. Box 2000, University Station
Enid, OK 73702

Oregon

University of Oregon
Department of Germanic Languages and Literature
Eugene, OR 97403

Portland State University
Division of Continuing Education
1633 S.W. Park
P.O. Box 1491
Portland, OR 97207

Portland Community College
12000 S.W. 49th Avenue
Portland, OR 97219

Pennsylvania

University of Pennsylvania
Department of Germanic Languages and Literature
745 Williams Hall
Philadelphia, PA 19104-6305

University of Pittsburgh
Language Acquisition Institute
Pittsburgh, PA 15260

Rhode Island

Brown University
Program In Swedish
c/o German Department
Box 1979
Providence, RI 02912

South Dakota

Dalsborgsföreningen
c/o Dalesburg Lutheran Church
Box 74, Route 2
Vermillion, SD 57069

184 AMERICAN-SWEDISH HANDBOOK

Texas

University of Texas at Austin
Department of Germanic Languages
Scandinavian Studies
Batts Hall 216
Austin, TX 78712

Rice University
Department of German and Russian
P.O. Box 1892
Houston, TX 77251

The Swedish Club
1612 Waugh Drive
Houston, TX 77006

Utah

Brigham Young University
Department of Germanic and Slavic Languages
4096 Jesse Knight Humanities Building
Provo, UT 84602

Virginia

University of Virginia
Department of German Languages and Literature
108 Cocke Hall
Charlottesville, VA 22903

Washington

University of Washington
Scandinavian Department
Raitt Hall, DL-20
Seattle, WA 98195

Pacific Lutheran University
Scandinavian Area Studies Program
Tacoma, WA 98447

Scandinavian Language Institute
3014 N.W. 67th Street
Seattle, WA 98117

Swedish Club, Inc.
1920 Dexter Avenue North
Seattle, WA 98109

Nathan Hale Community Night School
10750 30th Avenue N.E.
Seattle, WA 98125

Tacoma Community College
Continuing Education
5900 South 12th Street
Tacoma, WA 98465

Distance Learning
U W Extension GH-23
University of Washington
Seattle, WA 98195

The Language School
YMCA Building
909 Fourth Avenue
Seattle, WA 98104

Wisconsin

University of Wisconsin - Eau Claire
Department of Foreign Languages
Hibbard Humanities Hall 378
Eau Claire, WI 54701-4004

University of Wisconsin - Madison
Department of Scandinavian Studies
1366 Van Hise Hall
1220 Linden Drive
Madison, WI 53706

University of Wisconsin
Fox Valley Center
Division of Continuing Education
Midway Road
Menasha, WI 54952

Vasa Order of America
c/o Lillemor Horngren
8035 South Mona Drive
Oak Creek, WI 53154

RESOURCES

Newspapers and Periodicals
By Eric R. Lund

Swedish-American Newspapers

Only six of the hundreds of Swedish-American newspapers once published still remain. Of these, only two—sister publications *California Veckoblad* and *Svenska Amerikanaren Tribunen*—are full size. Three—*Norden, Nordstjernan Svea* and *Vestkusten*—are tabloid, while the sixth, *Swedish Press,* changed in 1986 to a monthly magazine.

The number dwindled to six in the late 1970's with the demise of three papers with long histories. *Svenska Posten* of Seattle, established in 1885, ceased publication in 1976 after the death of Henry F. Fabbe, its editor for 46 years. Enoch Peterson and Glenn D. Peterson discontinued their *Western News of Denver* in 1979 after 54 years of ownership. *Texas Posten* also died.

Svenska Amerikanaren Tribunen is still published almost entirely in Swedish, as is *Norden,* the paper for Swedish Finns. *Nordstjernan Svea* and *Swedish Press* have successfully broadened their appeal in recent years to reach wider audiences. Still, total circulation of the remaining papers is probably no more than 20,000.

In general, the papers publish news and feature articles from Sweden together with news of Swedish-American organizations. The area focus of *Veckoblad* is Southern California; of *Nordstjernan Svea,* the East Coast; of *Swedish Press,* the Pacific Northwest; of *Tribunen,* Chicago and Minneapolis, and of *Vestkusten,* San Francisco and the West Coast.

California Veckoblad
Established 1910. Mary A. Hendricks, Chief Editor; Jane A. Hendricks, Business Manager. Eight pages twice a month, 3 pages in Swedish. $15 per year ($25 to Sweden). 10921 Paramount Boulevard, Downey, CA 90241.

Norden
Established 1896. Erik R. Hermans, Editor. 8 pages tabloid. Weekly each Thursday (except last week in July, first two weeks in August and last week in December). For Swedish-speaking Finns. In Swedish, except for a few items in English. $20 per year ($25 to Europe). 123 W. 44th Street, New York, NY 10036.

Nordstjernan Svea
Established 1872. Alvalene P. Karlsson, Editor; Erik R. Hermans,

Production Editor. 16 pages tabloid. Weekly each Thursday (except last week in July, first two weeks in August, and last week in December). In English and Swedish. $32 per year, $18 for half year. 123 W. 44th street, New York, NY 10036.

Svenska Amerikanaren Tribunen

Established 1876. Jane Hendricks, Publisher and Editorial Director. 12 pages twice a month. In Swedish, except for a few items in English. $18 per year ($30 to Sweden). 10921 Paramount Boulevard, Downey, CA 90241.

Vestkusten

Established 1886. Barbro Sachs-Osher, Publisher; Bridget Stromberg-Brink, Managing Editor; Karin W. Person, Editor Emeritus. In English and Swedish. $20 per year ($30 to Sweden). 237 Ricardo Road, Mill Valley, CA 94941.

In addition to these publications another source of news about Sweden is the news sheet *Sverige-Nytt/Swedish-Digest,* written entirely in Swedish intended for Swedes aboard and for foreign readers who want to follow developments in Sweden.

Sverige-Nytt/Swedish Digest

Since 1948. Gunnar Miles, Chief Editor and Publisher. 8 pages weekly. $86.50 per year (Kr. 630). Hypoteksvägen 10, S-126 44 Stockholm, Sweden.

General Interest Magazines

Changed in format and frequency and expanded in coverage, *Swedish Press* moves from the Newspaper category to that of General Interest Magazine. The magazine, *Sweden Now,* published in Stockholm in English, French, German and Italian, ceased publication in 1989.

Sweden & America

Since 1987. Christopher Olsson, Editor. 24 pages quarterly (Winter, Spring, Summer, Autumn). News and articles about Sweden and Swedish-America. Subscriptions: $7.95 per year ($10 foreign), or with membership in many Swedish Council of America affiliate organizations. 2600 Park Avenue, Minneapolis, MN 55407.

Swedish Press
(Nya Svenska Pressen)

Since 1929. Anders Neumueller, Editor; Hamida Neumueller, Assistant Editor. 40+ pages monthly. News and features; focus on, but not limited to, Pacific Northwest; some items in Swedish. $17 per year (U.S. or Canadian). 1294 W. 7th Avenue, Vancouver, BC, Canada V6H 1B6.

Organization Periodicals

Many Swedish-American organizations publish a newsletter for their members. The following are among the most widely circulated, one *(ASI Posten)* regionally, the others nationally.

ASI Posten

Publication of the American Swedish Institute. Editor: Janice M. McElfish. 12 pages, 11 times a year. Free with ASI membership. 2600 Park Avenue, Minneapolis, MN 55407.

Gult och Blått i Boston och New England

Independent quarterly newsletter founded in 1980 for the Swedish-speaking community in New England. Editor: Sylvia Bullock. $10.00 per year, $19.00 for two years. Gult och Blått, 50 Pine St., Wellesley, MA 02181.

Musiktidning

Since 1905. Official journal of the American Union of Swedish Singers. Editor: Dan Olch. 8 pages monthly (except July and August). $8 per year. Suite 712, 333 N. Michigan Avenue, Chicago, IL 60601.

Svithiod Journal

Since 1898. Official publication of the Independent Order of Svithiod. Editor: Betty Jane Clausen. 8 pages monthly. $1 per year. 5518 W. Lawrence Avenue, Chicago, IL 60630.

Vasa Star

Since 1908. Official publication of the Vasa Order of America. Editor: Alvalene P. Karlsson, PO Box 1353, New York, NY 10028. Circulation Manager: Cynthia B. Erickson, 50 S.E. Bush Street, Issaquah, WA 98027. 24 pages monthly (except for combined issue July-August). $5 per year.

Viking Journal

(Formerly *Vikingen*)

Since 1901. Publication of the Independent Order of Vikings. Editor: Barbara Lou Upstrom. 8-16 pages monthly. $1 per year. Suite 257, 2200 E. Devon Avenue, Des Plaines, IL 60018.

Quarterly Journals

Journals of interest to Swedish-Americans range from *Scandinavian Studies,* which traces its history back 80 years to 1911, to Nils William Olsson's *Swedish American Genealogist,* which marked its 10th anniversary in 1991.

The Bridge

Since 1962. Erik Gustavson, Editor. 32 pages quarterly. Focus on emigration research. Diaries, letters, stories, etc., written by emigrants are often published, as are reader contributions. There is also an edition in Swedish: *Bryggan.* Free with membership ($8 per year) in the Society for the Promotion of Emigration Research. Box 333, S-651 08 Karlstad, Sweden.

Scandinavian Review

Since 1913. Adrienne Gyongy, Editor. 96+ pages quarterly (March, June, September, December). Articles and fiction reflecting Scandinavian culture plus news of art and design books, film, and music. $15 per year, or with membership in the American Scandinavian Foundation, 725 Park Avenue, New York, NY 10021.

Scandinavian Studies

Since 1911. Steven P. Sondrup, Brigham Young University, Managing Editor. 140 pages quarterly (Winter, Spring, Summer, Autumn). Scholarly articles on Scandinavian languages and literature, history, society, and culture. $40 per year, or with membership in the Society for the Advancement of Scandinavian Study, c/o Secretary-Treasurer, Virpi Zuck, Department of Germanic Languages and Literatures, University of Oregon, Eugene, OR 97403.

Swedish American Genealogist

Since 1981. Nils William Olsson, Editor and Publisher. 48 pages quarterly. Articles and essays on Swedish-American biography, genealogy, and personal history as well as methodology; lists of Swedish immigrants, books reviews, and questions from readers. $20 per year. PO Box 2186, Winter Park, FL 32790.

Swedish-American Historical Quarterly

(Formerly *Swedish Pioneer Historical Quarterly*)

Since 1950. Raymond Jarvi, Editor; Byron J. Nordstrom, Associate and Book Review Editor. 48-64 pages (January, April, July, October). Articles on various aspects of Swedish-American history, immigrant letters and diaries, news items, book reviews, and book notes. With membership ($25 per year) in the Swedish-American Historical Society, 5125 N. Spaulding, Chicago, IL 60625.

Swedish Book Review

Laurie Thompson, Editor, c/o St. David's University College, Lampeter, SA48 7ED Wales. Twice a year (Spring and Autumn).

Reviews, articles about authors, and excerpts from current Swedish books, with a supplement devoted to single author each Autumn. $22 per year by air to U.S. (in 1990). Subscriptions: Valerie Gustaveson, 260 E. San Jose Avenue, Claremont, CA 91711.

Facsimile (fax) News

The new technology of facsimile transmission has led to the development of a new medium for Swedish and Swedish-American news: facsimile or fax newswires.

Daily Swedish Newswire

Bengt Göransson, Editor, DSN Communication, Inc., 7320 Ohms Lane, Minneapolis, MN 55439. Tel. (612)942-8851; fax (612)942-8844. Faxed weekdays. Available in either Swedish or English. Emphasis primarily on business and trade with brief news items of more general interest. $295/six months plus transmission costs.

Sweden & America *is published quarterly by Swedish Council of America.*

Access to books and libraries

By Mariann Tiblin

Americans of Swedish descent and Swedes living in America have many options when it comes to finding literature about Sweden, whether about "the old country" or about current affairs in Sweden of today, or new novels, travel books and children's books.

Buying New Books from Sweden

The American book stores and importers listed below keep a selection of new Swedish books in stock, both in Swedish and English. In addition, some are willing to special order individual titles from Sweden. College bookstores at colleges with Scandinavian programs are also good sources for Swedish books and books about Sweden. Special ordering through an American outlet is the advisable option for the occasional book buyer. Ordering directly from a Swedish bookseller is also a possibility, although payment can sometimes be a complicated process for individual customers. (International money order or Mastercard/Visa is preferred to personal check. In each case it is advisable to inquire with the individual bookstore before sending order and/or payment.) Unlike what is common in the United States, ordering directly from a publisher is not customary in the Swedish booktrade; individual customers are usually referred to a bookseller. A practical way to facilitate regular bookbuying is to take advantage of the discount and shipping service offered to members by the *Riksföreningen Sverigekontakt* (The National Association for Contact with Sweden, see page 159) with headquarters in Göteborg, to which The Swedish Cultural Society in America is affiliated. The special needs of language teachers, libraries and others with an academic interest in Sweden are met through the services offered by the Swedish Information Service in New York and the Swedish Institute in Stockholm (see addresses on page 23). Visitors to Stockholm will find a wealth of information about all aspects of Sweden in many languages in the Sweden bookshop located in the *Sverigehuset* (Sweden House) near Kungsträdgården.

Finding Out What Is New

The Swedish booksellers offer jointly a handy illustrated annual guide to trade publications entitled *Årets böcker*. It is available free from bookstores and publishers. Eagerly anticipated every year in February is the sale catalog for the annual book sale which takes place simultaneously across Sweden: *Bokhandelns Stora Bokrea* (The Booksellers' Great Sale), which offers books from the publishing of recent years at substantial price reductions. Swedish books in Finland are listed in the annual trade publication *Finlands svenska böcker.* The Swedish Council of America quarterly magazine *Sweden & America* carries a regular column of reviews of new books about Sweden and Swedish-American relations.

Those with access to Swedish newspapers (sold at some international magazine stores in larger cities and available at the consulates general and in the libraries of institutions with Swedish instruction) will find current literary criticism and book notices on their cultural pages, a well established tradition in Swedish journalism. Book reviews in Swedish newspapers and magazines can be identified through monthly and annual indexes published by Bibliotekstjänst AB in Sweden (available in all Swedish libraries and in larger reference libraries in the United States). The ASI Bokhandel in Minneapolis is one outlet for Swedish books whose staff maintains direct contact with book distributors in Sweden. They plan to start publishing a mail order catalog in the near future, and they are also able to procure regional maps.

For specialized study, there are a number of journals and bibliographies available for subscription and in libraries.

Swedish literature in translation is presented in the British journal *Swedish Book Review,* published in Lampeter, Wales, by The Swedish-English Literary Translators' Association. American Scandinavianists publish reviews in the academic journal *Scandinavian Studies.* Of special interest to those involved in Swedish-American history are book reviews in *The Swedish-American Historical Quarterly,* which also includes an extensive annual bibliography in its October issue, and *The Swedish American Genealogist.* The Swedish Information Service publishes an annual list of New Books in the Reference Library of The Swedish Information Service with predominantly English language materials in all subject areas.

Finding Old Books

The antiquarian book trade in Sweden is represented by well-established firms in the major cities as well as by a growing number of second-hand bookstores all over the country. Many publish regular catalogs of books in stock, often devoted to particular subject areas such as biography, art, regional history, and the graphic arts as a service to collectors as well as to the occasional buyer. A list of antiquarian booksellers in Sweden is available from the *Svenska antikvariatföreningen* (Swedish Antiquarian Boksellers' Association), and they can also be found in the phone book's yellow pages under *"Antikvariat".*

Some American antiquarian and out-of-print booksellers in this country are listed below.

Subscription Services

In addition to the free newsletters and brochures available at the Swedish Information Service, the Swedish consulates, the Swedish Tourist Board, and the Swedish Institute, commercial subscriptions to magazines, journals, and newspapers can be ordered through major export firms such as Esselte/Almqvist in Stockholm and Munksgaard in Copenhagen, who will handle subscriptions from all Scandinavian countries.

Libraries, Reference, and Information Services

The Swedish Information Service in New York maintains a reference library and a telephone and walk-in reference service, and is the foremost clearinghouse for all types of information needs related to Sweden. For historically oriented research as well as general reference, the academic libraries at institutions with Swedish roots and at those offering Scandinavian programs (see page 166) provide extensive collections of Swedish books collected, in many cases, for over a century. Those libraries also maintain newspaper and periodical collections of considerable depth, as well as national and subject bibliographies, databases, and information in electronic format. Interlibrary loan of books and photocopies of periodical articles can be dispatched to any public, academic, or participating private library in the country and facilitated by their reference departments. The collected resources of American research libraries in most areas of the humanities and social sciences often match those of libraries in Sweden, whereas current popular literature, magazines, and children's books are less prevalent in American libraries and best sought in the book stores.

Business and law literature pertaining to Sweden is also available at the major university and college libraries. For current information in these areas contact the Swedish Information Service, the Swedish consulates, or the Swedish-American Chamber of Commerce and their regional affiliates.

Many research libraries maintain special collections of particular interest to the Swedish-American history researcher. In 1986, the University of Minnesota acquired the Tell G. Dahllöf Collection of Swedish Americana. The collections of the Swenson Swedish Immigration History Research Center are now located in splendidly refurbished quarters in Denkmann Library at Augustana College, and those of the Swedish-American Historical Society on the campus of North Park College in Chicago have also recently been moved into new and expanded space. On the West coast, the collections at Pacific Lutheran University are being preserved for the future, and in Philadelphia the American Swedish Historical Museum specializes in the early history of the Swedes in

America.

The archives of institutions with Swedish roots include, in addition to manuscripts, photographs, and other unpublished materials, extensive collections of older Swedish and Swedish-American books, as well as microfilms of archives and newspapers, and oral history recordings. For a directory to archival repositories see *Guide to Swedish-American Archival and Manuscript Sources in the United States* (Chicago: Swedish-American Historical Society, 1983). The guide is updated periodically with news items in the *Swedish-American Historical Quarterly*. For specific information on repositories and current projects please refer to the archives at the Swenson Swedish Immigration Research Center at Augustana College in Rock Island and at the Swedish-American Historical Society at North Park College in Chicago.

Of special interest to genealogists are the collections of books and microfilms in the Family History Library in Salt Lake City with their network of branch libraries in major cities. Access to Swedish church records in microform is now possible through the genealogical research service at the Swenson Swedish Immigration Research Center in Rock Island which serves as U.S. distributor for the SVAR (Svensk Arkivinformation) records of the Swedish regional archives. The libraries and archives of state historical societies often contain material of Swedish-American interest, particularly in states with heavy influx of Swedish immigrants. Those libraries can in turn be helpful in identifying collections in county and city historical societies.

What To Do With Old Books

Many Swedish-American individuals and sometimes smaller institutions face the question of how to dispose of old Swedish books. Larger and specialized libraries will sometimes accept old books as gifts, and antiquarian book dealers will buy books in certain subject areas and in good condition. For larger collections, it is advisable to seek an outside evaluation by a professional appraiser.

Dealers

ASI Bokhandel
The American Swedish Institute
2600 Park Avenue
Minneapolis, MN 55407
(612) 871-4907
Fax (612)871-8682

The Swedish Book Nook
P.O. Box 1343
New York, NY 10028
(212) 744-8224

The Swedish-American Museum Center
5211 North Clark
Chicago, IL 60640
(312) 728-811

Glada Grisen, Inc.
489 Woodlawn Avenue
Glencoe, IL 60022
(708)835-1096
Fax (708)835-1404

Melvin McCosh, Bookseller
26500 Edgewood Road
Excelsior, MN 55331
(612) 474-8084
(Old books)

Lien's Bookshop
57 South 9th Street
Minneapolis, MN 55415
(612) 332-7081
(Old books)

Esselte Bokhandel
Almqvist & Wiksell International
Post Office Box 62
S-101 20 Stockholm
SWEDEN

Hemlins Bokhandel
Vasterlanggatan 6
S-111 29 Stockholm
SWEDEN

Sweden Bookshop
Sweden House
Box 7434
S-103 91 Stockholm
SWEDEN

Svenska Antikvariatföreningen
(Swedish Antiquarian Booksellers Association)
Box 22549
S-104 22 Stockholm
SWEDEN

Akademiska Bokhandeln
Post Office Box 128
SG-00101 Helsinki 10
FINLAND

Munksgaard
N. So/gade 35
DK-1370 København
DENMARK

GEOGRAPHICAL INDEX
OF ORGANIZATIONS

Nebraska

Gothenburg

Scandinavian Heritage Group, 95

Holdrege

Tre Kronor Scandinavian Society, 142

Lincoln

The Norden Club of Lincoln, 77

Society for the Advancement of Scandinavian Study, 99

Oakland

Oakland Chamber of Commerce, 81

Swedish Heritage Center, 132

Omaha

Noon Day Scandinavian Club, 76

Scandinavian-American Society, Inc., 87

Swedish Cultural Committee, Inc., 125

Vasa Order of America - Iowa-Nebraska District Lodge #17, 147

Stromsburg

The Swedish Festival, 130

Wausa

Vasa Nordic Club, 144

Nevada

Las Vegas

Vasa Order of America - Valhalla Lodge #715, 151

New Jersey

Basking Ridge

Vasa Order of America Youth Club - New Jersey District #6, 148

Bridgeton

New Sweden Farmstead/Museum, 75

East Orange

Upsala College, 175

Woodcliff Lake

SWEA International, New Jersey Chapter, 109

New Mexico

Albuquerque

Nordic Dancers of Albuquerque, 89

Northland Dancers (Children's group), 89

Scandia Dancers, 89

Scandinavian Club of Albuquerque, 88

Scandinavian Summerfest, 98

Svenska Klubben, 104

Uff da Band, 89

New York

Beechhurst

Manhem Dancers (Folk Dancing), 73

Bronx

Manhem Club, Inc., 73

Buffalo

SWEA International, Buffalo Chapter, 109

Franklin Square

Svenska Societeten, 105

Hartsdale

Society Åland, 99

Jamestown

American Scandinavian Heritage Foundation, 37

Jamestown Community College, 171, 182

Norden Club of Jamestown, 77

Norden Women's Club, 78

Viking Male Chorus, 46